Collectors' Guide to
MODEL AERO ENGINES

O. F. W. Fisher

Model and Allied Publications,
Argus Books Ltd,
14 St James Road,
Watford, Herts

Model and Allied Publications,
Argus Books Ltd,
14 St James Road,
Watford, Herts,
England

Text and illustrations © O. F. W. Fisher
© 1977 Argus Books Ltd

ISBN 0 85242 492 2

All rights reserved.
No part of this publication
may be reproduced in any form
without the prior permission
of Argus Books Ltd.

Printed and bound in Great Britain by
Hazell Watson & Viney Ltd, Aylesbury, Bucks

CONTENTS

	Page
Foreword	4
List of illustrations	5
Introduction	8
1 Compressed Air Engines	13
2 Petrol Engines	15
3 'Slag' Engines	25
4 Diesel Engines	27
5 Multi-Cylinder Engines	48
6 CO_2 Engines	55
7 Pulse Jet Engines	56
8 Horizontal Piston Engines	57
9 Mock Engines	58
10 Jetex Rocket Engines	59
11 Electric Motors	60
12 Glow Plug Engines	61
13 Replica and Semi-collectors' Engines	71
14 Propellers	74
15 Fuels	76
16 Timers, Tanks and Plugs	78
17 Operating Tips	81
18 Cleaning, Overhauls and Restoration	83
Glossary of Technical Terms and Abbreviations	86
Plates	90
Index	130

FOREWORD

THE SCOPE of this subject is so great, that to enable the finished work to be concise and of the maximum use and interest to the reader, many engines and points of interest have had to be treated in a very cursory manner, or even omitted altogether.

The engines selected to illustrate the text have been chosen, with a certain bias towards the unusual, to provide examples of the gradual design and development of the model aero engine from its inception to the present day.

An effort has been made to show how the engines have been designed for various specialised types of model aircraft. Each engine is a dynamic mechanism, the subject of much design work and careful constructional and metallurgical techniques. They reflect the ideas of the men that designed and built them; and are equally varied in character and function.

The primary purpose of this book is to try to pass on a little of the pleasure to be derived from the study and use of these engines; and to show how their diverse characters are evolved through a multiplicity of selective compromises at all stages in their evolution. It is sincerely hoped that the end product will be of the maximum interest to the greatest number of people, and that everyone will find something of specific interest to himself.

Acknowledgements

The author would like to thank his many friends and associates for their help and encouragement in the writing of this book; and in particular the following individuals, who have supplied information or photographs.

R. Leisses, D. Peugh, H. Whal, J. Law, T. Ten Brink, P. Scott, K. Harris, P. Ross, Doc Nichol, K. Carlson, G. Buck, R. Ashby, J. Kemp, M. MacLean, L. Saxby, A. Imrie, R. Raddon, P. Chinn, R. Polglase, S. Persson, A. Allbon, F. Acat, G. Ginns, G. Rawlings, R. Reuter, R. Hetherington, C. Juby, J. Kloth, S. Cannizzo, G. Nurthen, S. Wagstaff, P. Smith, K. Fisher, H. Hilscher, G. Hargrave, J. Mayes, P. Emerson, J. David-Andersen, J. Jessop, G. Pearce, P. Whitworth, A. Cross, D. Jones, E. Keen, Little, Curtiss, B. Lane, N. Morita, M. H. H. Hobbs, Northfield-Ross, K. Bartram, Moteurs Micron.

LIST OF ILLUSTRATIONS

Serial numbers are given where applicable and page numbers are given for those illustrations which do not appear in the plate section at the end of the book.

Fig.
1. Hoosier Whirlwind A. (p. 14)
2. Brown Brownie P. (29E13) (p. 14)
3. O. & R. ·60 SP, P. (028374) (p. 14)
4. Hallam 10 P. (p. 14)
5. Bunch Warrior P. (p. 14)
6. Bunch Aero Mighty Midget P. (p. 14)
7. Brat ·14 & Model L. P.
8. Mechanair 5·9 P.
9. Atlas 3·5 P.
10. GHG 4·4 P.
11. Lyon MP 5 P. (186)
12. Lyon MP 10 P. (25)
13. K 6 P. (1289)
14. Hurleman ·48 P.
15. Performance Kits Model L.
16. Smith Lapwing P. (356)
17. Clipper Sky King P.
18. Condor Kopper King P.
19. Dennymite ·573 P.
20. Baby Cyclone P. (F10929)
21. Anderson Spitfire ·65 P. (6100 Series)
22. Micron ·29 Super Sport G.
23. Stentor 6 P.
24. 1066 Falcon P.
25. Majesco 4·5 P. (420)
26. O & R FRV ·23 P. (47671)
27. O & R ·23 SP
28. Vivell ·35 P.
29. Arden ·199 BR P.
30. Super Hurricane ·24 P.
31. Queen Bee ·23 P. (0038)
32. Strato ·604 P.
33. Super Cyclone P.
34. Westbury Kestral P.
35. Delong 30 P. (38580)
36. Atom Minor 6 cc P.
37. Pierce ·29R & Forster ·29 (Right)
38. Hetherington ·23 P.
39. Perky P.
40. Howler ·604 G

Fig.
41. Atom Super ·09 P.
41A. Atom 1·8 replicas (35 produced)
42. May Rocket ·56 P. (21)
43. Rocket Victor P. (8856)
44. Contestor D60R. P.
45. Gannet Aero P.
46. Morton M–5 P.
47. Thor ·29 P. (p. 26)
48. Dyno D (p. 26)
49. Rawlings 18 D (143)
50. Rawlings 30 D. (147)
51. Owatt 5 cc. D. (D251)
52. Drone Bee D. (11404)
53. Vivell ·06 D.
54. Strato ·604 D.
55. Ouragan ·9 cc. D.
56. Airstar 2·15 D. (19–725)
57. ED Mk. 2 D. (C/122/8)
58. Bensen-Thorning D. (014)
59. Majesco Mite ·735 cc. D
60. Mills Mk 1 series 2 D. (40)
60A. Mills Mk 1 series 1 D. (16–61)
61. Mills Mk 2 D. (36–595)
62. Mills ·75 Mk 2 D. (51/992)
63. Mills 2·4 D. (45/486)
64. Performance Kits Bonnacon.
65. GHG 10 cc Twin P.
66. GHG Mk 1 2·44 D.
67. GHG Mk 2 Production batch.
68. GHG 4 cc G.
69. Micron M2-24 'Bi-cylindre' G(876) (p. 54)
70. Amco Mk 1 ·87 D. (2769)
71. Amco PB 3·5 D. (2798) Ser 1
72. Amco PB 3·5 D. (133) Ser 2
73. Frog 1·75 P.
74. Frog 100 Mk 2 D. (14907)
75. Frog 1·49 Vibromatic D. (4475)
76. Frog 50 Mk 1 D.
77. Frog 80 D. (9869)

Fig.
78. Frog 1500 Viper (1608)
79. Kemp 4·4 cc D. (522)
80. K Eagle D. (388)
81. K 1·9 D. (762)
82. Kemp Hawk ·2 D. (1601)
83. K Kestrel 1·9 cc (K449)
84. K Falcon 2 cc D. (233)
85. K Vulture Mk 1 (126)
86. K Vulture Mk 3 D. (3009)
87. ED Comp. Special D. (K141–9C)
88. ED Bee Mk 1 D. (IF 61 751)
89. ED Baby Mk 2 D. (DF 55 32)
90. ED Hunter D.
91. ED Racer Mk 2 D. (RM 130 51)
92. ED Super Fury D.
93. ED Bee Mk 2 D. in PK Apex
94. ED Miles Special D. (p. 70)
95. ED Pep D.
96. ME Heron D. (p. 70)
97. McCoy ·049 D.
98. Elfin 1·8 C/L D.
99. Elfin 1·8 F/F D.
100. Elfin 2·49 D. Radial
101. Elfin 2·49 Mk II D. (Q4144)
102. Elfin 2·49 BR D.
103. Taifun Hurrikan D.
104. DC Wildcat Mk 3 D.
105. DC 350 Mk 2 D. (4347)
106. DC 350 Mk 2 G. (1915)
107. DC Manxman D.
108. DC Rapier Mk 1 D.
109. HP Mk 3 D. (D–218)
110. Comet Mk 1 D.
111. Eta 5 cc D. (44894)
112. Osam D. (60873)
113. Super Tigre G.32 D.
114. Super Tigre G.30 D.
115. David-Andersen Drabant Mk I D. (7138)
116. David-Andersen Drabant Mk II (1972)
117. David-Andersen Satellitt D.
118. Typhoon R-250 BR D. (38)
119. Typhoon 5 cc BR D.
120. Atom IA D. (0319)
121. MVVS 1·5 cc D. (213)
122. P.A.W. 249-DS D. (1975)
123. Pfeffer 0·6 cc D.
124. OTM Kolibri 0·8 cc D.
125. Motop Mk 16 D. (72-1005)
126. Vertorek 0·5 cc D.
127. Rhythm (Ritm) D. (696)
128. Taipan 1·5 D. in PK Apex
129. Rivers Silver Arrow D.
130. Zom 2·5 BR D. (D1294)
131. JB Atom 1·5 cc D.

Fig.
132. Deezil D.
133. Embee ·75 Mk I D.
134. Embee 10 D. (In Airmaster.)
135. Embee Mk IV D.
136. Embee Flat Twin Mk 1 D.
137. Jena 1 cc D.
138. Jena 2 cc D.
139. Jena 2·5 R/C D. (p. 70)
140. Taifun Hobby Mk 1 D. (X-AD-Mk 3)
141. Taifun Hobby Mk 2 D. (35131)
142. Taifun Rasant II D. (10119)
143. Micron Meteor ·9 cc D.
144. Micron 2·5 Racing D.
145. A-M. 25 Mk 1 D. (1437)
146. Super Sokol BR D.
147. Apex Nipper D.
148. Saxby ·375 & 0·5 cc D.
149. Fisher 3·5 D.
150. Speed Demon 30 D. (135 5)
151. OK Herkimer Twin P. (60941)
152. Wasp Twin P. (3263)
153. Viking 65 P. (1504)
154. Craftsman Twin P. (80901)
155. Elf Flat Four
156. Pal ·55 Twin P.
157. FMO Little Boxer D.
158. PK Panther V-Twin D.
159. Typhoon 7 cc Twin D.
160. Rupert Boxer Twin. D.
161. D-C Tornado Twin G.
162. Ross in-line ·60 R/C G.
163. Ross Flat Twin G.
164. Ross Flat-4 G.
165. Ross Flat-6 G.
166. Wizard ·65 Twin G. (1300)
167. Micron 2-24 G.
168. Micron 4-24 R/C G. (p. 54)
169. FMO Boxer 7·5 (p. 70)
170. Kamikaze ·40 R/C Twin G. (p. 54)
171. Allyn Sky-Fury Twin G. (p. 54)
172. Brown Junior CO_2
172A. Telco CO_2 Prototype in modified PK 'Owl'.
173. Dyna-Jet, OS Jet & Sona Jet (p. 56)
174. Aero ·35 G. (p. 57)
175. Embee ·75 Mock Rotary D. (p. 58)
176. Lionheart Mock Twin D. (p. 58)
177. Jetex 200 (p. 59)
178. Hetherington Meteor ·23 G.
179. Frog 160 G. (2451)
180. Frog 500 G.
181. Exeter 10 cc G.
182. OK Cub ·19 G.
183. DC Wasp ·049 G.
184. Atwood ·049 Cadet G.

Fig.
185. O & R Midjet G.
186. Gilbert ·07 G.
187. Viking 2·5 G.
188. Pagco Pagliuso XF-9 G.
189. Johnson Stunt Supreme G. (PK Pinnacle Mk E-54)
190. Yulon ·30 G.
191. Yulon ·29 G. (29/439)
192. Yulon Eagle G.
193. K & B ·201 G.
194. Glo-Chief ·35 Mk 2 (Eclipse Mk 48)
195. Glo-Chief ·35 BR (Lynx Mk 15) G.
196. PK 'Oclet', powered by Telco Co_2
197. Micron Meteor 51A C G.
198. Nordec RG 60 G. (427)
199. Dooling ·61 B Series G. (1785)
200. Rossi ·60 G.
201. Komet ·15 G.
202. BMP 3·5 D.
203. HP Mk II P. (M544)
204. Telco CO_2
205. Favoriet 2·47 D. (S67)
206. PK 'Capital–L' powered by Cameron ·23 SP
207. Tono ·35 R/C G. (2708)
208. Micron ·35 R/C G. (Sun Bird)
209. Micron ·45 R/C G. (Sun Bird)
210. Micron ·21 G.
211. Remco ·29 P. (285)
212. Doonside Mills ·75 D. (288)
213. Indian Mills ·75 D. (AH138)
214. Propeller Collection (4 Photos)
215. Khobe Rhino G. & Moki 25 cc (p. 73)
216. Cameron ·23 SP. P. (4941) (p. 73)
217. Mystery Engine (p. 73)

Fig.
218. Etha 2·5 cc D.
219. Majesco 4·5 P. Restoration
220. Hobbs ·75 cc D.
221. OK ·60 P.
222. BE-961 6·2 cc (1941–46) twin D.
223. Micro 0·8 cc D.
224. Cannon 300 P.
225. Hornet ·19 G.
226. ORR Tornado ·65
227. Streamline 6 P.
228. Hurlerman Twins P.
229. DC Bambi D. (Right)
230. Mills ·75 Mk 1 D.
231. Bunch Tiger Aero P.
232. McCoy ·29 P.
233. Cloud Elf Models, powered by Atom 1·8 and Airstar 2·15 at 1965 Nats.
234. Majesco 4·5, before restoration
235. PK Cloud Mini-Elf, with Kemp ·2
236. East German Metro 2·47 cc D.
237. MECA Region 13 Meeting—summer 1975
238. Taipan 2·5 BB R/C G.
239. PK Cloud Elf—Airstar 2·15
240. A-S ·55 (1960) D.
241. Bantam ·60 Twin R/C G.
242. PAW 1·49, 2·49, 19-D, 19-BR
243. Dragon 16 (M. E. Bastable Ltd, Wimbledon) P.
244. Airplan 5
245. Bos Morin 3·5 cc D.
246. PK X-ULT D.
247. M-S 2·5 cc Eccentric D.
248. PK Greater Duster (Stentor 6)

INTRODUCTION

In the year 1896 Professor Langley built and flew what was probably the first power-driven model aircraft to fly consistently and successfully. This model used two pusher airscrews rotating in opposite directions to neutralise torque effects and was fitted with a steam engine. The model was catapult launched from the roof of a houseboat and flew for half a mile over the Potomac River in America. The duration of this flight was 90 seconds. Professor Langley also built the first petrol powered model to fly. His original petrol powered machine flew 300 ft in 10 seconds. Much later, in 1903, the first man-carrying machine was flown under power by the Wright brothers.

Some of the first commercial model aero engines were made in England by Mr D. Stanger, who produced several multi-cylinder petrol engines for specific model aero applications in 1907. These included a V4 four-stroke unit. This remarkable engine drove a two foot diameter propeller at 1300 rpm and developed about 1·25 bhp. It had push rod operated overhead intake valves and automatic exhaust valves. At the time, it was claimed to be the lightest 4-cylinder engine in the world and weighed 86 oz without ignition equipment. This early engine allowed Mr Stanger's bi-plane to take-off at 16 mph when fitted with a 29 inch × 36 inch propeller. Wingspan of the model was 8 ft 6 inches. This V4 was followed, in 1914, by a Stanger V-Twin, and using this engine, he established the first official power driven model aero record with a flight of 51 seconds, which was unbroken for 18 years. His next engines were an in-line 4-stroke 3-cylinder petrol motor and a 15 cc in-line 3-cylinder 2-stroke.

In 1910 A. W. Gamage Ltd of London marketed a 25 cc single cylinder petrol engine, which weighed 3 lb including its trembler coil. It was sold complete with a gravity feed petrol tank.

The first American commercial engine was perhaps the Baby Engine of 1911. Weight was $\frac{3}{4}$ lb and $\frac{1}{2}$ bhp was claimed. The advertised cost was $35 and the motor was manufactured in Stamford, Connecticut.

In 1912 Stuart Turner Ltd made two petrol engines, one a single cylinder and the other a flat twin.

It is worth mentioning that a number of Flash Steam engines, for use with model aircraft, were available at about this time. A later 3-cylinder development of one of these engines, designed by Mr F. J. Camm, claimed ·2 bhp at 1500 rpm with a large diameter propeller. All up weight, including fuel, water and oil, was quoted at ·875 lb.

The first mass-produced motor was probably the Brown Junior ·601 cubic inch which was marketed in large numbers from 1934 and it is from this period forward that the commercial model aero engines, dealt with in this book, were put into production. Before this, however, the compressed air motor had a brief period of popularity.

1 : Compressed Air Engines

THESE ENGINES formed a link between the first rubber powered model aircraft and the commercially produced 2-stroke petrol engines. They date back to about 1900.

By 1910 several English compressed air engines were available to the aeromodeller and could be purchased from Stevens Model Dockyard in London. These engines were available in 2, 3, 4, and 6 cylinder form and were rotary engines. It is interesting to note that the same firm also sold clockwork units for powering model aircraft.

The Nomie Engine Co. Ltd of Chicago were the first to market a compressed air engine in America. The 1911 Nomie was of the popular 3-cylinder type and was similar to English design practice. It may even have been manufactured in England. Weight for this unit was $6\frac{1}{4}$ oz and it produced ·25 bhp at 2500 rpm. Air pressure tubes could be purchased separately and affixed to the engine. Later air engines usually had their air reservoirs filled with a pump. It is probable that the name Nomie was derived from the full size Gnome rotary engine.

Joe Ott, in 1929 produced, in conjunction with the Amalgamated Sales and Service Corporation of Chicago, motors with $\frac{1}{2}$-inch bore and a $\frac{5}{8}$-inch stroke in 3, 4, and 6 cylinder forms. He also designed the Ott featherweight flat twin, produced by the Norlipp Co. Frontal diameter, including pipes, was 6 inches. Over 800 of these engines were eventually sold. The Ott Favorite was a 3-cylinder engine and two of these motors could be arranged to form the 6-cylinder model.

Later came the Dob-Ott air motor, only available in 3-cylinder form and introduced in 1930. Early examples had a spun front shaft housing. The Dob-Ott weighed $2\frac{1}{2}$ oz and had a bore and stroke of $\frac{1}{2}$ inch. Induction was via a shaft rotary valve.

Other well known compressed air engines were the Imp Japanese V4 Dry Ice engine and the German Autoplan 3-cylinder engines; these were popular for some years, while the Aston 3-cylinder engine had an interesting ball type valve operated by a push rod and cam drive from the crankshaft. The Aston weighed $1\frac{1}{4}$ oz and exhaust is via holes drilled in the cylinder wall just above the piston crown at bdc. The ball was located in the inlet port where the air feed pipe entered the top of the cylinder. The crank web was counter-balanced.

Many other air engines were made; but the Hoosier Whirlwind (Fig. 1) 3-cylinder, with $\frac{3}{8}$-inch bore and stroke is a typical example of the better type of commercially produced unit. The motor illustrated is a replica of this engine, recently produced by Oldtimer Models of Milwaukee, Wisc. The air tank, made of thin gauge brass, was used to double as the model's fuselage and was frequently wound with wire for extra strength. This was blown up with air from a pump. A tap controlled the air outlet and ducting to the tops of the pistons. On the Whirlwind the con-rods are of stamped brass about $\frac{1}{32}$ inch thick. Power/Weight ratio for these motors was low and the performance of the models was rarely up to the standards of a rubber powered machine. With the introduction and general availability of the miniature model aero petrol engine, the compressed air engine passed into history.

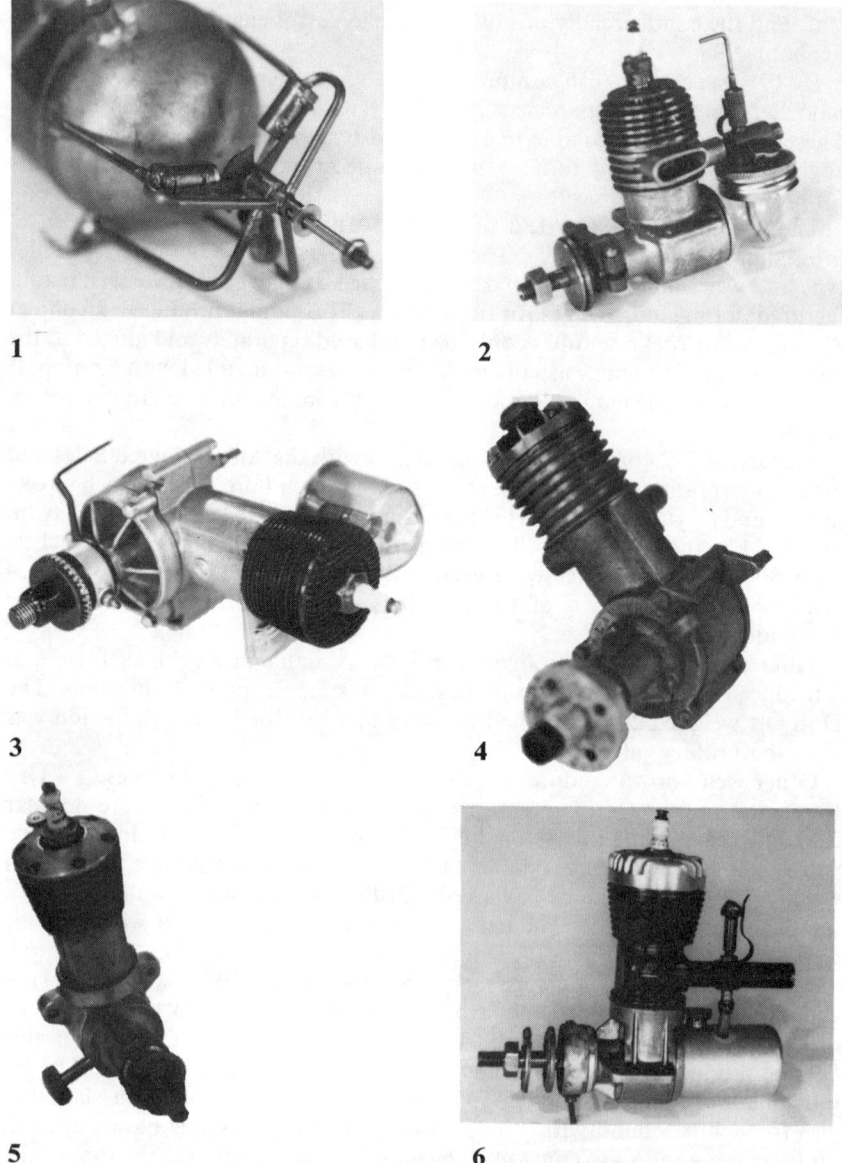

1

2

3

4

5

6

2 : Petrol Engines

(1) Side Port

MOST commercially produced Model Aero Motors were, and still are, of the 2-stroke type and it is felt that the design progression to date has been almost equal in all fields, notably: Metallurgy, Bore/Stroke Ratio configurations, porting layouts, timing and constructional techniques. In order to place the engines in a reasonably orderly progression and allow for the fact that different configurations were in production simultaneously in different countries, the engines are being grouped by induction systems, as this is one of the most obvious means of differentiating between them. In England before World War 2 many side port engines, such as the 1933 Grayson Gnome 3·5 cc and Greyspec 15 cc, which weighed 16 oz, were in production; but the earliest engine, with the greatest production record was the American built Brown Junior ·601, which was introduced in 1934. It was of the side port configuration. This is sometimes erroneously called the 'three port type'. The idea is that there is one port for induction, one for transfer of fuel mixture and one for exhaust. It can be seen that the nomenclature is incorrect, as even with the Brown, the 'transfer port' is sub-divided with the fuel mixture travelling through several apertures to the combustion chamber. Thus the term 'side port' (SP) will be used in this book. The Brown Junior had a bore of $\frac{7}{8}$ inch and stroke of 1 inch. Power was quoted at $\frac{1}{8}$-inch bhp at 4500 rpm with a 14-inch propeller. On September 13, 1932, a model fitted with the prototype of this engine set an official world endurance record of 13 minutes 53 seconds at Atlantic City and reached a height of 3000 ft.

It is a little known fact that the first twenty Brown Junior engines made in 1934, and known as the Model A, were in fact constructed by Walter Hurleman Inc. in Philadelphia. The motors were an immediate success and led to the subsequent founding of Junior Motors Inc. Mr Hurleman then left the company and produced his own, very similar, Hurleman ·60.

In 1940 Brown Junior Motors produced a ·29 side port called the Brownie (Fig. 2). The ignition advance and retardation was adjusted by moving a cast arm through an arc on the front of the crankshaft housing. A cam on the back of the prop driver disc bears on a spring to which the moving point is duly attached. The point is spring loaded in the open position, and is closed once in every rotation of the prop driver. The fuel jet was fixed, but a needle valve could be adjusted, so that its tapered point progressively closed the jet opening. Air was drawn in through the open ended intake tube, subsequently vaporising fuel due to the needle valve restriction over the jet and the resultant mixture entering the inlet port. This simple induction system was used on most side port petrol engines.

A number of examples are given. Fig. 3 illustrates a 1945 Ohlsson and Rice

·60 Special. When arranged for inverted running, as shown, a special fuel tank top cover was supplied as an extra. This enabled the spring loaded tank filler valve to seat correctly. The engine illustrated is serial number 028374. Fig. 4 is a pre World War 2 Hallam 10 cc, manufactured in Poole, Dorset. The specimen illustrated is minus its contact breaker assembly. A 1938 Bunch Warrior ·451 cubic inch motor is illustrated in Fig. 5. The motor was designed by Dan Bunch and had a power output of $\frac{1}{8}$-inch bhp at 5500 rpm. The large knurled knob on the point retaining housing allows the timing to be locked as required. The Warrior was fitted with two piston compression rings, and was only made in the radially mounted form shown. The crankcase is gravity cast. It originally sold for $12. Fig. 6 shows the 1946 Airo Mighty Midget, another Bunch design, of ·451 cubic inch displacement. This engine is similar in appearance to the Contestor D60S. J. Keener designed the 1937 Brat ·138 cubic inch (Fig. 7). The specimen shown is, in fact, an exact replica, using mainly original parts, and produced in 1972 by Mr Karl Carlson of Replica Engines in San Jose, California. The 1946 Mechanair 5·9 cc Red Head (Fig. 8) was built in Birmingham and was developed from the earlier Flat Head Astral 5·9 and subsequent, almost identical Mechanair Black Head model. The Atlas 3·5 cc (Fig. 9) was a very well built small petrol engine from the same makers as the HP Mk 2 3·5 cc (Fig. 203). The GHG 4·4 cc (Fig. 10) was manufactured in Coventry in 1938; it is interesting to note that the spark plug was also of GHG manufacture. The MP Lyon 5 (Fig. 11) and MP 10 (Fig. 12), which have serial numbers 186 and 25 respectively, are both of similar layout, except that the 10 cc model features a rear exhaust port. Both use $\frac{3}{8}$-inch diameter Lodge spark plugs. The K6 (Fig. 13) was introduced just after World War 2, the example illustrated being serial number 1289. It originally sold for £8 17s 6d (£8·87$\frac{1}{2}$) including coil condenser and propeller.

An interesting variation on the standard side port theme is the 1946 Hurleman Aristocrat ·488 cubic inch (Fig. 14). This engine incorporated a collar type fuel adjuster instead of the usual needle valve. As the collar was screwed in, so it effectively covered the fuel jet opening. It worked well, but was slightly more critical to adjust than the traditional needle. The knurled end of the collar has a friction spring to bear on it and so provide a 'click' adjustment. The engine illustrated was completed in 1972 by Herb Wahl from original castings and parts. In 1938 Mr Hurleman started the ·48 series of engines. The first ones had a single exhaust, which was subsequently enlarged and finally gave way to the twin exhaust model.

All the early side port engines were designed for use in Free Flight models and Fig. 15 shows a Brat ·14 installed in a sports type F/F semi-scale model, the Performance Kits Model-L, of 50-inch span.

Ignition was usually by means of the traditional coil and condenser with 3–4·5 v. battery ignition; however a few engines, such as the Gerald Smith Lapwing (Fig. 16) which was made in Nuneaton, England, incorporated a built-in magneto. The engine shown is serial number 356. The motor is fitted with a 'clapper' type throttle, and a separate shaft, under the crankcase, carries the effective contact breaker friction mechanism.

Another side port engine, with self-contained ignition, was the Hugh Gunter designed Generator Clipper, which had its own built-in generator affixed to the rear cover plate. Only about half a dozen were made. The project was terminated by the introduction of the glow plug. Fig. 17 shows the Clipper Sky King, which is an orthodox version of the same engine, with a displacement of ·381 cubic inch. All Clipper models were produced in 1951. The most common version was the Clipper XX770, which was the same as the Sky King, but used a metal tank. It is believed that only a thousand of all types of Clipper were produced.

In November 1941, the Condor Kopper King was introduced. Capacity is ·604 cubic inch and weight $7\frac{3}{4}$ oz (Fig. 18). It will be seen that the advance and retard mechanism is arranged so that it can be adjusted from the rear of the engine, so keeping the fingers away from the prop disc. The head and the top five fins were solid copper. The cylinder and remaining fins, transfer cover and exhaust stack were steel. They were brazed together and copper plated. The overall effect is very pleasing. The point cover is of black Bakelite and a red fuel tank is fitted. The rear crankcase cover is machined and stamped with the makers name. Early Kopper Kings had a bronze con-rod, while later models used a steel forged one. A few engines were produced after 1945, and these can be recognised by the two-letter prefix to the serial numbers. The pre-war models only had a single letter 'A' prefix. American entry into the war in December 1941 terminated the project prematurely.

The Dennymite, designed by Mr W. Righter was manufactured by the Righter Mfg Co. for Reginald Denny, a film star, and was produced from 1937–41. Fig. 19 shows the last model manufactured for Mr Denny in 1940. It is of ·573 cubic inch capacity. Later models were manufactured by the Pacific Automotive Corp.

The largest capacity mass-produced side port engine was the 1946 Avion Mercury 45. Bore was 1·25 inches and stroke 1·312 inches, giving a capacity of 1·609 cubic inches. It bore a considerable resemblance to the Forster ·99. The Avion, thanks to magnesium castings only weighed 20 oz. $\frac{3}{4}$ bhp at 4000 rpm was claimed with a 20-inch × 10-inch propeller. The engine was fitted with a barrel type throttle, which was the forerunner of todays R/C motors. Price was $57·50. Production ceased in 1947.

In general, front rotary shaft induction boosted power output, an early example was the 1938 Baby Cyclone Model F of ·364 cubic inch capacity (Fig. 20) produced by Aircraft Industries. The model illustrated is serial number F10929. The crankshaft had a port cut in it and was drilled through to the inside of the crankcase, along the shaft axis. The Baby Cyclone was also one of the first engines to use a spray-bar type needle valve assembly. The spray-bar ran right through the venturi intake. It was a hollow tube with a small jet hole or holes drilled in it. One end of the tube was connected to the fuel line, while the other was threaded to take the needle, either internally, or mounted to an external collar. Early engines, such as the Baby Cyclone used the first method, while a collar type came into fashion later.

With the introduction of rotary shaft induction, power outputs increased and the engines became more sophisticated. Look at the Anderson Spitfire in Fig. 21. This ·604 cubic inch engine was manufactured in 1947 by the Mel Anderson Mfg Co. and featured a ball-race crankshaft and superb die-castings. It was advertised as 'The Cadillac of Model Engines'; a claim which was well justified. This engine was much favoured for early radio control models. It was designed by Mel Anderson who produced many excellent motors. The engine shown is the 6100 series model.

The front rotary did not suddenly surplant the old side port engines however and both types remained in production by many different manufacturers well into the post–1945 period; indeed there are examples such as the Doonside Mills ·75, which were available in 1974. In 1946 the Bunch Contestor D60S 10 cc side port was performing excellently in company with such motors as the Anderson Spitfire, Super Cyclone and Orwick ·64, although the Orwick was always considered to be the most powerful engine in its class. All these motors were greatly favoured in early C/L models in about 1947. The wing area of a C/L stunter, designed for the Contestor D60S, such as the Eclipse Mk 6 was 500 square inches. By comparison, in 1960, a Micron ·29 sport stunt engine (Fig. 22) was used in the Performance Kits Pinnacle illustrated which had a wing area of 580 square inches and a vastly superior performance! It is interesting to record that while flying the Contestor 60 powered Eclipse Mk 6 model in Kensington Gardens, London, in 1950, the early plastic Tru-flex propeller disintegrated in flight, but the engine continued to run with its substantial crankshaft acting as a fly-wheel!

In general, engines produced in America, had a superior external finish to British and Continental motors. This was largely due to the far greater production figures for the American motors, which were often produced in a ratio of perhaps a 1000:1 to their British and Continental counterparts. The British engines, as a rule, were relatively more expensive, and often represented more than a week's wages, for the average man before World War 2. For this reason a great deal was expected of these British-built motors. Piston/bore fits were hand lapped, and great care was also taken with the fits of all moving parts. Crankcases on the other hand were usually simple sand-castings; due to the previously mentioned low production volume and consequent lack of funds for expensive die-castings. Some excellent English-built engines illustrating these points were motors such as the 1946 Stentor 6 cc, which was produced in Poole, Dorset (Fig. 23), the G. Smith Lapwing (Fig. 16) and the Hastings 1066 Falcon (Fig. 24), which features a very superior brazen exhaust manifold; all of which featured sand-cast crankcases; but had good tolerances on working surfaces.

After World War 2, British engines began to incorporate die-cast crankcases. Such motors were produced by Reeves, Majesco Motors, with the 4·5 cc (Fig. 25), which was produced in 1946, and the Atlas 3·5 (Fig. 9), which was produced by Hobby Products in Barnet, Herts. One of the last production British side port petrol engines was the 1946 5·9 cc Red Head Mechanair (Fig. 8), which was made in Warwick Road, Birmingham and for which ·2 bhp was claimed.

During the same period in America, a vast number of side port engines were in production although these were mainly of pre-war design; however in 1968 the Golden Eagle ·53 cubic inch SP petrol engines were produced in small quantities by Spielmaker Engines. Priced at $45, to make a new side port engine available for vintage model aero flyers and collectors.

The Cameron ·23, from Senora in California, was in production both before and after World War 2 and a late example (No. 4941) is shown in Fig. 216. It is a very well built SP unit, with attractive grey stove-enamel finished crankcase. The overall design is similar to the O & R ·23, but workmanship is generally superior. The motor is of much more robust construction.

(2) Shaft Rotary Valve

In general, the front shaft rotary valve (FRV) engines tended to outperform the side port models. Firms such as Ohlson & Rice tended to redesign earlier side port units to FRV; but otherwise they show a strong family likeness (see Figs 3, 26, 27). The short crankshaft bearing length was a weak point with these motors, but they were top sellers and gave good power for the price paid. The motor shown in Fig. 26 is the 1946/7 O & R ·23 FRV model serial number 47671, while Fig. 27 features a 1940 O & R ·23 side port. A ·23 SP won the South Coast Gala in a Halifax Spartan before World War 2.

Other FRV engines in production at the same time were the 1946 Vivell ·35. Fig. 28 shows a 4th series model. Another was the very powerful and lightweight 1947 Arden ·199 cubic inch ball race motor (Fig. 29) designed by Ray Arden of Micro-Bilt Inc. This was the first engine to incorporate the radial transfer port system, in which multiple transfer flutes were cut with a broach. The Arden crankcase is pressure die-cast in magnesium alloy, and features radial mounting. A neat plastic fuel tank is fitted underneath, and the general standard of workmanship and finish is of a very high order. The power/weight ratio of this engine, when in production was unsurpassed.

The fuel mixture is induced via an inlet port, cut in the hollow part of the crankshaft. Fuel enters this port via an intake tube, which is fitted, often as part of the crankcase casting, but sometimes through a separate induction tube; either upright, as with the Super Hurricane 24 (Fig. 30), downwards, as with the Baby Cyclone (Fig. 20) and Arden (Fig. 29) or, on the side, as with the Cannon engines. The Cannon also had an unusual cylinder head featuring concentric cooling fins.

Most model aero engines employ a cast crankcase with a detachable rear cover as with the Brat 14, or a detachable front crankshaft housing, as with the O & R range. Some early petrol engines split the crankcases vertically down the sides, as with the Hallam Nipper; others, such as the 1937 Husky, produced by Homer Conklin, were composite. The Husky Junior and subsequent 1938 Bat engines had vertically split lower crankcases with orthodox superstructures. A similar system was used for the rare Fireball 500, made between 1937–45 by the Acuntra Tool & Die Company of New York. This latter engine also had some other unusual features. The intake tube of this SP motor was curved to face forward, and this, together with its radially finned head and tank were of brass. Capacity of the engine was ·79 cubic inch. A 1·57 cubic inch V-twin was also produced.

From Canada came several excellent engines. The Queen Bee ·24 (Fig. 31) was made by Mr Al Salonen in Vancouver, BC between 1945–7. At one time this engine held the West Coast class speed C/L record at over 100 mph. Total production of all types of Queen Bee engines was under 400 units. Approximately the first fifty were ·24 cubic inch and the remainder were ·29 cubic inch. The engine illustrated is serial number 0038, and has had the contact breaker assembly removed, as it has been operated as a glow-motor. To determine the difference, inspect the crank-pin. The diameter is $\frac{3}{16}$ inch for the ·24 cubic inch model and $\frac{1}{4}$ inch for the ·29 cubic inch model. The first engines to be produced had no serial numbers; then about 150 engines were serial numbered up to about 200, and the remainder were again numberless. Mr Salonen made about 5 or 6 diesels and one each ·60 glow and petrol engines of the FRV type, which are in the collection of Canadian Collector Mr R. Polglase.

One of the first FRV engines was the Baby Cyclone (Fig. 20), which had the distinction of having the cylinder head retained by its $\frac{3}{8}$-inch diameter spark plug. Probably the most common Canadian engine was the Super Hurricane ·24 (Fig. 30). It was designed by Ray Hunter and built in Toronto. The motor illustrated is the 4B series of 1948 manufacture. Various models were made between 1944–9. The unusual cylinder head finning was intended to provide extra cooling for the rear of the head; but actual benefits were largely stylistic.

A relatively limited production Canadian engine was the excellent Strato ·604, which although of side port configuration has been included as an example of high class Canadian model aero engine production. The example shown in Fig. 32 belongs to Mr J. Law of Newark (courtesy P. Emerson). The Strato engines were made by Mr Randall Bainbridge during World War 2. The first production engines had cast iron cylinders and heads with radial fins. Weight, however, was 15 oz and to reduce this the next model had an alloy cylinder with iron liner; at the same time a more traditional head was incorporated with milled parallel fins. Before production stopped a few prototype FRV induction engines were made; but the motor was out-priced by various American products, such as the Super Cyclone (Fig. 33), which again became available after the war.

The Super Cyclone was available in both single and dual plug versions, and is illustrated in the latter form. The motor bore a strong design resemblance to the Anderson Spitfire (Fig. 21), although the Anderson was in fact the superior motor.

(3) Disc Valve Induction

The disc valve is usually associated with the racing type of engine, such as the Dooling ·61, Hornet ·61, Rossi ·61 and the Nordec ·60, which were all of the rear disc valve type. A disc of aluminium alloy or fibre is driven from the rear end of the crankshaft.

One of the earliest motors to use this type of induction was the Westbury Kestrel (Fig. 34) designed in 1937 by Edgar T. Westbury in England. This unusual motor incorporated a very thin disc driven from the front of the crank-web. The air intake faced forward and the fuel feed line was incorporated in the crankcase casting. It featured what Westbury described as a 'Port Belt'. This casting incorporated the exhaust and transfer passages and pressed on the centre of the cylinder. The idea was to simplify construction, should the engine be built up from castings.

Rear disc valve engines include the excellent DeLong ·30 (Fig. 35). The engine illustrated is serial number 38580. It was made by Super Motors Inc. The much earlier E. T. Westbury designed new Atom Minor 6 cc (Fig. 36). The example illustrated was machined from castings by Mr L. Saxby, and is of excellent workmanship. The original Atom Minor was one of the very earliest engines to feature rear disc induction and was of advanced design when first introduced. Westbury also produced the much earlier 15 cc Atom Minor, which features a ball race crankshaft, in its final form. This was of course a side port motor.

From Cleveland, Ohio, came the Barker Man-ul-matic described by the makers, the Barker Engineering Co., as the 'Wonder Motor of the Model World', and while this is perhaps an overstatement, it was certainly a very interesting engine and 65 separate components make one such engine! The two castings used are both of magnesium. Induction is via a disc rotary valve. On turning the engine anti-clockwise and putting pressure on the rotary shaft the crank-pin moves to a secondary position on the rotary valve disc, where it is located by a spring; by this means the intake port opens earlier, the object being to obtain a greater charge for starting. When running, pressure is again applied via the control and the crank-pin is allowed to slip to its running position. The engine was made to a high standard throughout and each engine was neatly labelled with an enamelled maker's nameplate.

To conclude this chapter, there was one engine which had both rear disc rotary and side port induction combined. This was made in very small numbers in 1951. And is known as the Sampson ·30. The crankcase, finished in grey, was from a Pierce petrol engine. There were two Pierce engines. The R type used rear disc induction and the J type was a side port. Both engines used the same crankcase casting and bore a strong resemblance to the Forster 29 (Fig. 37). The engine illustrated is the late model, fitted with a metal petrol tank and two-speed timer. The Pierce was a less expensive motor than the Forster and was not built to the same high standards. The Sampson 30 used both types of Pierce induction in one engine!

(4) Clack Valve Induction

Mr R. Hetherington built his first engine in 1932 in Los Angeles and used the name Meteor from 1935. The 1939 Hetherington Meteor ·23 cubic inch

(Fig. 38) side port motor is a truly remarkable and unusual engine. It features a spring loaded clack valve. A thin metal disc with scalloped edge is interposed between the intake tube and a locating ring at the rear of the crankcase; the entire assembly being held in place with a locking collar. This disc opens and closes with the pressure differential between the atmosphere and the inside of the crank-case, so metering the induction charge.

In many ways the Hetherington Meteor is quite unique. Instead of the usual cast crankcase, this component, together with the front housing, engine mounts, timer arm, prop driver and even the cylinder fins are shaped from sheet metal. The cylinder fins are then brazed in place. The crankcase is fabricated from 13 steel stampings! Workmanship is of a very high order throughout. Every engine was factory tested before despatch.

Another American engine using the clack valve induction system was the Perky. The original Perky was introduced in 1940. Fig. 39 shows the pre-war model on the right and the post-war model on the left.

(5) Sub Piston Induction

An exceedingly interesting engine was the Howler ·604 (Fig. 40). The engine shown is in the D. Peugh collection, which had air taken in by sub-piston induction, as its only air intake; there being no air intake at the needle valve. The engine was in limited production and is now a much sought-after collector's item.

The twin ball race Howler ·604 cubic inch engine, designed by Mr L. Fowler was produced by the Bone Tool & Gauge Co. of Detroit in 1946–7. The model illustrated being of 1946 manufacture. About 300 of these engines were made altogether.

Fuel was taken in through the crankshaft centre line drilling and entered the crankcase via two opposed egress points on the crank-web. In 1947 Howler produced a second model, which in fact had a very small air intake at the needle valve, but this only accounted for a small proportion of the air induced.

An interesting sidelight is that the engine was originally designed to fly a model helicopter as a rescue marker for use in rubber life dinghies for the US Navy. The helicopter was to be tethered to the lifeboat by a cable. The company was in fact tooled for production of these engines at $50 each; but the contract was cancelled with the termination of the war.

Every Howler was bench tested to run up to 18,000 rpm before despatch. The FOB price was $34·95 when new.

(6) Valve-in-Piston Induction

The smallest commercial engine of its time was the little 1941 Atom Super ·09 from Micro Dyne (Fig. 41) using the above type of induction, together with a fixed fuel jet opening and variable air intake, which was operated by a long lever. The Atom's valve-in-piston induction replaced the usual transfer port type induction system.

The motor was designed pre-World War 2, but was available in Mk 2 form in 1946, when the Capitol Pixie was produced for it. This was a class A cabin F/F model with a span of 40 inches and polyhedral wings. Early Atom motors had circular multiple exhaust ports.

Another engine employing the valve-in-piston type induction system was the rare American M & M.

(7) Drum Valve Induction

In 1940 May Motors of Detroit produced the May Silver King ·451 cubic inch, selling at $16·50. The rear induction drum ran inside the fuel tank, so promoting their claim to be a 'Liquid Cooled Carburation System'. Bore was $\frac{7}{8}$ inch and stroke $\frac{13}{16}$ inch. May Motors was cast on the exhaust stack. Two holes were drilled through the crank web to aid counterbalancing.

Fig. 42 shows the 1941 May Motors Rocket ·56 cubic inch, serial number 21, which was originally advertised at $17·50. Fig. 43 features the Rocket Victor, serial number 8856, which was produced by Corporate Products Inc. and sold for $22·50. This model was of ·451 cubic inch capacity. Both used the same die-castings except that the name on the exhaust stack was changed from May Motors to Rocket Motors.

Externally the die-cast components are clean and rugged and the engines run well. Inside we see a stamped con-rod fixed to the piston with a steel yoke, bolted through the piston crown. The counterbalanced crank-web is also stamped and force fitted to the end of the crankshaft. The end of the crankpin drives the induction drum via a thin steel rotating drive arm, which is held to the end of the drum by a key held in position. The drum itself runs inside a housing formed by the cast rear cover plate of the engine. The carburettor casting is produced by Autolite on the Rocket Motor. The earlier May Rocket used the fabricated plastic unit illustrated in Fig. 42.

The last Rocket motor to be produced was the 4610 model introduced in 1947, which went out of production in 1949. This 4610 model was also known as the Model C and is in fact the same engine. Production was still by Corporate Products Inc. of Detroit who sold this model direct from the factory at $8·95 in 1947. It was claimed that 30,000 had been sold. This model had enclosed contact points and the tank was a separate entity, being in fact a car carburettor float. The 4610 model had a new hexaganol carburettor housing for the venturi.

Fig. 44 features the very powerful Contestor D60R drum valve engine designed by Dan Bunch and made in 1946 by Lucas & Smith. The piston was suitably ringed and the cylinder head deeply finned and incorporating a $\frac{3}{8}$-inch plug. The side port model, from the same firm, was known as the D60S.

(8) 4-Stroke

Such engines as the English Gannet, produced by Gannet Engineering Ltd in Whitstable, Kent, have overhead valves and are of 14·98 cc. One of the rare aero-versions is shown in Fig. 45. An 18-inch × 6-inch or 22-inch × 5-inch propeller is recommended and magneto ignition could be specified as an extra. Lubrication was of the displacement type, using cup-feed. The name Gannet was derived from the name of the engine's designer Mr G. A. Nurthen. The engine could still be obtained to special order in 1970. A 30 cc ohv twin was also available.

The American Feeney from Chicago (known as the Feeney 4-cycle) and the Morton-Burgess (Fig. 46) both use the 4-stroke layout. This latter engine was firstly produced by the Morton Mfg Co. in Omaha, Nabraska, and later by the Burgess Battery Co. The photograph shows a 1945 M-5 ·92 cubic inch model. It is of 5 cylinder radial construction, $5\frac{3}{8}$ inch overall diameter, incorporating a distributor at the rear together with external push-rods and rockers. $\frac{1}{4}$-inch spark plugs are used. Bore is ·625 inch and stroke ·600 inch. The picture shows a new example, complete with its variable pitch alloy propeller and mounting brackets. Half bhp at 3500 rpm was claimed. In use it was found that a 14-inch × 6-inch propeller was preferable.

The Morton M-5 was low on power for its size and weight of 22 oz; but possessed about the same output as a modern ·29. We recently tested one in a semi-scale R/C bi-plane. Power was marginal but the engine note was a delight to the ear and the model performed a loop, after a slow climb to aerobatic height. Capacity was ·92 cubic inch and power $\frac{1}{2}$ bhp at 3500 rpm.

Another 4-stroke production engine was the 10 cc Channel Island Special. It was made by J. & G. Jensen Ltd and had enclosed overhead valve gear.

One of the earliest English 4-stroke petrol motors was the Grayson 25 cc and 30 cc. Both were made by E. Gray & Son in Clerkenwell Rd, London, in 1933 and were fitted with overhead valves. The advanced specification included many Elektron castings, comprising the two-piece crankcase and valve guides. The 30 cc version stood 7 inches high and weighed 4 lb 2 oz. Bore and stroke were both $1\frac{5}{16}$ inch. As well as producing complete motors, these engines could also be purchased as a casting kit, for the home machinist.

In 1975/6 the Hargreave 5- and 7-cylinder 4-stroke motors were made, firstly in Cirencester and subsequently in Ireland. Most of these radial type quality units have been exported to Japan. All are glow ignition.

3: 'Slag' Engines

THIS singularly appropriate term has been given to certain engines by collectors and relates to engines which leave a certain amount to be desired in design and quality of construction. Specifically a lack of cylinder liner.

A good example is the 1946 Thor ·292 cubic inch, produced to sell for a very low price and marketed as the AHC Super model (Fig. 47). The engine has no cylinder liner, so that the piston runs directly in the blind bored cylinder unit. Two bolts, with Phillips heads, hold this unit to the crankcase. The contact breaker is of the 'wipe-swipe' type. A piece of greased cardboard, crimped to the back of the prop driver, has an opening cut in it, which allows contact to be made with the contact-breaker arm. The low tension circuit is broken when the contact points run over the cardboard insulator!

The Genie was a slightly improved version of the Thor, with a new timer and tank, and with the fins machined round.

Other Slag engines are the Rogers, Buzz, Judco and Ram, together with various Synchro engines, produced by Synchro Devices. This firm had previously produced the well thought of and interesting Synchro Ace ·56 cubic inch in 1937, together with the ·122 cubic inch Bee and Ace Special ·56 cubic inch in 1938. The Ace featured an unusual streamlined crankcase and tank. Synchro Devices Slag engines commenced with the Synchro B-30 and the Synchro PC-2, which was an alternative version of the B-30. Although these engines are not among the world's most desirable units, there are engine collectors who specialise in them for their curiosity value. They are certainly not highly recommended for flying purposes.

When in production these engines were very inexpensive, selling for $3·95. Vast numbers were sold on the American market.

Mr C. Rogers produced the various Rogers engines in Philadelphia, starting in 1941 with the side port KD-29 from the Rogers Motor Co.; although the engines were actually manufactured by the Judson Company of the same city. The 1941 Rogers ·29 and ·35 were similar to the KD-29, but were adapted from side port to front rotary shaft induction. In the process the old side port induction passage was blocked off and fitted with a dummy induction tube, which was simply used to suspend the fuel tank. A fuel tube then connected this tank to the FRV intake. For further effect, the timer drum and tank were finned to match the head. All Rogers engines used 'V Alloy', which is believed to be an Aluminium/Zinc alloy, and dispensed with cylinder liners, to their great detriment.

The last pre-war Rogers engine was the RMC-2 (Rogers Motor Co.), which was very like the earlier KD-29. In 1946 the FRV Rogers ·29 was introduced featuring a stub rear air intake; and in 1947 the Rogers Ram ·29 used up the earlier side port engine parts, but had an improved contact breaker. Also in 1947, Judco, who made all the Rogers and Thor engines sold a very similar engine, which was marketed as the Judco Ram, and this engine was also sold as the Buzz B in 1948, by the American Hobby Center. The Buzz A, B and C motors still used the old KD-29 crankcase castings. There was also a Buzz D 10 cc, with a new casting, which is considered to be the best of the Buzz engines.

Another engine in this mass-produced category is the GHQ petrol engine, which was based on the much better quality all sand-cast 1933 Lautrel ·452 cubic inch motor. It should be noted however that the GHQ was in fact fitted with a cast iron cylinder barrel.

The English Milford Mite 1·41 cc was a diesel which left a good deal to be desired in many ways, and some consider that it falls roughly into the Slag category; although it in fact had a cylinder liner, and the engines would run.

The Drome Demon was one of the few genuine Slag engines made in Britain. The Mk 1 version was of linerless construction, and the external appearance of the crankcase had a rather 'clinker'-like appearance. The Mk 2 version was in fact fitted with a liner. The motor, which is only sought after by collectors, has recently been manufactured in replica form, to supply this market. The Demon was originally sold in Birmingham, through the Model Aerodrome, a well-known model shop with branches in Cherry Street and Stratford Road. The same firm also made the Drome range of flying model aero kits. The Demon was introduced pre World War 2 and was a very basic, low price, petrol motor.

47

48

4: Diesel Engines

OVER the years there has been considerable speculation as to who was the first to manufacture a model diesel engine. The credit is usually given to Klemenz-Schenk; however recent research has indicated that the first commercial motor may well have been the Swiss Etha engine. The examples shown in Fig. 218 were originally purchased by the Spanish Air Attaché in Geneva in 1941. They were subsequently brought to Barcelona in the same year. A number of Etha engines are still in existence. The more common one is the 2·5 cc model. The larger diesel exceeds 10 cc. To start the 2·5 cc it was necessary to heat the finless cylinder head with a blow-torch. Fuel entered the choke tube of this side port motor via a junction tube, at the end of which was the needle valve, and which in turn was joined by the fuel union. The jet was of the 'surface' type, where it joined the choke tube wall. The choke tube itself entered the side of the motor, opposite the exhaust port. A figure of 2500 rpm was quoted as the running speed for the motor! The larger Etha motor had a relatively orthodox N/V assembly, except that the needle was flattened on one side, and was not threaded into the spray bar, as it was a friction fit. Some Etha engines have the name Etha contained within a Swiss cross, as a trade mark. As late as 1946 the Etha 2 was in production, still without cylinder fins and with a capacity of 6 cc.

The first mass produced commercial diesel, or more correctly Compression Ignition engine, was probably the Swiss Dyno (Fig. 48) which was produced by Klemenz-Schenk in 1946. It was of the traditional side port type. This engine was much copied, and many similar engines soon appeared in Britain and on the Continent.

One of the first Italian diesel engines, showing a strong Dyno influence, was the 1946 Giglio 2 cc designed by Mr Grazzini in Florence. The crankshaft of this engine is fabricated from three pieces, welded together, which is unusual in Europe, where crankshafts, particularly for diesels, are usually machined in one piece.

In France, at about the same time, M. Debrel designed and manufactured the Delmo 2·65 cc side port. The original Delmo engines had bolt-on pressed covers fitted over the upper crankcase sides, which were pierced with three holes to allow for the egress of the exhaust gases. The series 2 version dispensed with these plates, which were strictly for appearance purposes only. The Delmo was probably the first French mass-produced diesel engine.

In England the Leesil, produced in Bradford, bore a very strong resemblance to the Dyno. It was produced in small quantities and was of 2·5 cc capacity.

Apart from using the basic induction systems explained in Chapter 2, diesel engines have four types of compression adjustment; the fixed head, which is set by the makers. Adjustment by contra-piston, which is either moved by the cylinder head itself as with the ED Mk 2 (Fig. 57) and Rawlings 18 and 30 (Fig.

49, Fig. 50) or through the medium of a compression vernier, which is the most common method. In America some Vivell and Bunch diesels used an Allen key adjustor in the cylinder head. The Vivell also had the unique design feature of placing the contra-piston in the cylinder head, rather than in the top end of the cylinder liner. The final methods of compression adjustment are the eccentric compression engines discussed in section 2, and by moving liner (see section 5).

(1) Fixed Compression

One of the first fixed compression diesels was the French Micron 5 cc. This was a well made front rotary shaft induction motor, which held many early model aero records. The almost identical Owatt 5 cc (Fig. 51) produced by Modella Engines of Bradford, Yorkshire, originally sold for 9 guineas (£9·45) including propeller, and featured a fuel tank incorporating a spring loaded cut-out. With all fixed compression diesels the fuel mixture is critical, as effective compression variation can be made by altering the oil content. Most Owatt engines had a red painted crankcase.

The American Drone Bee (Fig. 52) 5 cc was one of the few popular diesels in the USA and was used for early stunt C/L models. Several versions were produced and a 1947 ·297 cubic inch motor is featured in the photograph. The cylinder head is gold anodised, and the crankcase is black. It will be noted that the venturi is cast in unit with the front crankshaft housing. The Mk 2 version had a separate screw-in venturi unit and a ball-race crankshaft. The final model incorporated a variable compression head.

The other fixed head diesel from America was the early Vivell ·06 cubic inch engine which also featured a rotary disc rear induction (Fig. 53). The last version of the Vivell ·06 also featured variable compression, actuated by an Allen key.

From Canada came the largest fixed compression production diesels in the form of the side port Strato ·604, with detachable exhaust stack (Fig. 54).

Most engines made in the southern hemisphere were produced on a very small scale; such as the Pepperill engines of New Zealand. An exception to this rule is the prolific output from Gordon Burford, whose engines went into production in 1946 and continue to the present day. A vast number of different models have been produced and a complete book would be required to cover them in detail. Here are a few historical facts. Gordon's first commercial engines were a few 1946 Sparey 5 cc diesels, followed by about 250 examples of the Gee-Bee GB-50 5 cc fixed compression diesel called the Stunta-Mota; this bore a very strong resemblance to the American Drone. It was made from 1947–9.

Following production engines were the GB 50 front shaft rotary diesel with parallel fins above and below the radial exhaust ports and variable compression, together with its companion glow version the GB 50G, both of 5 cc. Next came the GB 75, a 7·5 cc glow, and the GB 250 2·5 cc diesel with combined radial and beam mounts. The above were produced in lots of about 250 each between 1947–9. At this time Gordon decided to change his trade name from Gee-Bee to Sabre. This name was derived from the words 'South Australian Burford Racing Engine'. Several excellent early stunt glow engines were then made. The name was then changed to Glo-Chief. In 1963 Performance Kits imported the first Glo-Chief engines into England; they were of ·35, ·29, and ·49 cubic inch capacities, and won many Stunt C/L competitions, including the Gold Trophy. Latterly Glo-Chief became Glow-Chief, with the introduction of further R/C motors.

In 1959 there was a further change of name, this time to Taipan, after the poisonous Australian snake of the same name. The first Taipan was the 1·5 cc diesel, bearing a family resemblance to the GB 250, and featuring combined radial and beam mounting, a red anodised cylinder head and locking compression bar.

There are a few themes running through Gordon Burford production engines. Firstly they were all front shaft rotary induction motors and secondly they had pressure gravity cast crankcases. Production was usually in lots of 250. Nomenclature is very difficult, as different engines were known by their capacity, An exception being the Taipan Tyro of 1·9 cc, produced in 1971. Nearly all engines imported into England were discontinued from production before the demand for them had been fulfilled.

(2) Eccentric Compression

The French Ouragan, made by R. Chatet in Paris was probably the first commercial engine to use this layout. A lever was keyed to an eccentric phosphor-bronze bearing, which in turn rotated in the crankshaft front housing of the crankcase. Thus by rotating the lever, the entire crankshaft con-rod and piston was raised or lowered relative to the fixed cylinder head, and the compression could thus be altered.

The disadvantage of the layout was that the transfer and exhaust ports were fixed and so the port openings were altered with compression variation; however for the long stroke, relatively low speed engines of the period, this method was very effective. Ouragan (French for storm) produced two models, the ·9 cc (Fig. 55) and a 3·36 cc which were similar in appearance. The larger engine turned a 10½-inch × 7½-inch propeller at 6600 rpm. The author's little ·9 cc Ouragan is seen in a X-AC-5 assymetric F/F flying wing, which has had many good flights to its credit.

The Airstar 2·15 cc (Fig. 56) was produced in High Town, Luton, Bedfordshire. It came with both a C/L and graduated F/F tank of smaller diameter. It was very reasonably priced when new, at £3·75. The Airstar used a fixed orifice jet and a threaded air-slug to vary the mixture. The model in Fig. 56 is a 1939 Cloud Elf of 52-inch span and is ideal for this engine. The Cloud Elf was originally designed for the Cloud 3 cc petrol engine.

A few Scottish Clan ·9 cc diesels were made, using eccentric crankshaft bearings, and there was also the MS 2·5 cc from Newcastle. This engine weighed 5¾ oz. It was radially mounted and featured a silver steel crankshaft and drop forged con-rod. Price was £6 10s 0d (£6·50). D/C produced a prototype, but it never went into production.

David Andersen in Oslo was one of the first to produce an eccentric compression diesel. This side-port unit of 2·5 cc was highly thought of, but few were made.

The French Airplan engines, were in fact the forerunners of the Airstar 2·15. After producing a 5·5 cc fixed compression diesel, they made a 2·15 cc unit, which was almost identical to the Airstar, except that the Airplan was fitted with a traditional type of needle valve assembly and a slightly different rear cover plate. Ace Models Red Ace kit, which was an early pylon type model, built by the author in 1947, was specifically designed for this rare motor, and was illustrated on the plan.

(3) Variable Compression by Rotating Head

One of the first production British diesels was the ED Mk 2 (Fig. 57). Today this engine is often referred to as the Penny Slot Model. The reason is that a slot was provided on the top of the cylinder head, into which a penny could be inserted to rotate the head, which in turn bore down on the contra-piston and so increased the compression. The engine illustrated is serial number C/122/8. The grooved prop retaining washer was incorporated, so that the motor could be started using a leather thong. This engine was the first production motor made by ED. They were often fitted with twin exhaust stacks.

After World War 2, there were numerous precision engineering companies throughout England that turned their attention to the manufacture of model aero diesel engines. Among these was G. W. Rawlings and Partners Ltd in Warwickshire. During the war they had produced precision gauges, and in 1948 two superb diesels were put into production.

Rawlings engines were all built to the highest engineering standards; and unlike many of the competitors, they were built up to a standard, not down to a price. Only two models were produced, the R-18 of 1·8 cc capacity (Fig. 49) and the R-30 of 3 cc (Fig. 50). Both models were of basically similar design, and were of the most aesthetically pleasing appearance.

The R-30 featured a Nitralloy 70-ton crankshaft, which was drilled and given a groove for lubrication purposes. The cylinder liner was also of Nitralloy, and was given an exhaust port on either side, with an induction port at the rear and a transfer port at the front. The passages for these were machined inside the top half of the crankcase, which also served to locate the liner, against a flange. Four bolts held the two halves of the crankcase together, and their heads were covered by the beautifully machined cylinder head, which was threaded to the top of the liner, and also served to adjust the compression. Compression adjustment was made by fitting a box spanner over the hexagonal top of the cylinder head.

All Rawlings engines had a unique feature. This was the patented contra-piston, which was made up of a three part sandwich. The top and lower section were mild steel, but the sandwiched section was of lead alloy. When the engine was cold, the contra-piston could easily be adjusted, but as it reached running temperature the lead expanded more than the steel, locking the contra-piston in place, and providing a gas-tight seal.

The rear crankcase cover plates were threaded in position with a special tool, leaving the cover plate completely free of the usual slots and tightening holes. This feature effectively prevented the engine from being fully dismantled. With the exception of the underside of the lower crankcase casting the entire engine was machined, and many parts were also polished. The fuel cut-out and prop driver were also blued.

The Rawlings 18 was similar in design and specification to the R-30, except that it was of smaller capacity, and had a hole drilled full length along the underside of the crankcase. The idea of this was that the engine could be fitted with a variable speed control, by effecting a crankcase bleed. One prototype was fitted with this feature, but it was not incorporated on the production engines.

Both engines, as can be seen from the above had every feature that was thought to be desirable, even when these features were sometimes in the nature of refinements, rather than essential to the running of the engine. For instance a dowel peg gave positive location alignment at the front of the cylinder liner, and the gudgeon pin was tapered and ground, to fit the Meehinite pistons.

Every engine was extensively factory bench tested. No R-30 left the works giving less than 44 oz static thrust. Many gave up to 48 oz. The R-30 developed ·27 bhp at 7500–8000 rpm, which was a very high output for 1948. Another factory test was to check that the R-30 would give a minimum of 7500 rpm on a 12-inch × 5-inch propeller.

The R-18 was factory tested to give a minimum of 7500 rpm with a 10-inch × 5-inch propeller. The minimum static thrust figure, in this instance, was 26 oz.

The author is the proud possessor of the last two Rawlings engines to leave the factory. The R-18 is serial number 143, and the R-30 is number 147. Mr Rawlings believes that these numbers represented the total output of each engine. In 1948 the R-30 retailed at £6 5s 0d (£6·25), and the R-18 at £4 17s 6d (£4·87½). These were ridiculously low prices for such superb engines, and compared with other cheaply made motors then in production. With the advent of purchase tax, the Rawlings went out of production.

George Rawlings, and his son Vincent are still running the company today, although they are no longer connected with the model trade, to the lasting detriment of the latter. Mr Rawlings and his son have given the author considerable help with this technical information which is gratefully acknowledged.

In 1947 the Danish egg-shaped Bensen-Thorning was being produced in small numbers at Snekkersten near Elsinore. Fig. 58 shows the unusual slipper type cylinder head, which dispensed with cooling fins. The engine illustrated is serial No. 014. The exhaust port faces forward and the liner is held down with a knurled collar. Fits are good and the engine runs well. It is interesting to note that the Bensen-Thorning was developed from the well-thought-of Danish 2·4 cc Monsun Standard, which was also designed by Leo Jeppesen and built in the same works. It is thought that the first diesel to be produced in Denmark was the Diesella, which was the same capacity of 2·4 cc as the Monsun.

The GP 1·5 cc side port, from Sweden, was named after its maker an Italian called Gian-Carlos Pinnoti. Production started in 1944. Early examples had a two-piece crankcase. The head was rotated by a neat ball-ended lever, which in turn varied the compression. In 1949 it was replaced by the GP1001 orthodox SP 1 cc diesel.

The Majesco Mite, 0·735 cc, which was produced by the Majesco Motors Company in Dorset, better known for their 4·5 cc petrol ignition side port, was a delightful little motor, and was very well made. It featured a radial mounting back-plate, and the carburettor assembly was mounted at right angles to the crankshaft, and featured an aluminium tank, turned from the solid. A compression lever fitted through a raised section at the top of the cylinder head, was used to rotate the entire head about the top end of the threaded cylinder. Very few Majesco Mite motors were made, and Majesco Motors concentrated on their 2·2 cc diesel. A brand new specimen of the Mite is shown in Fig. 59. Retail price was £3 19s 6d (£3·97½) and all up weight, including the fuel tank was 2oz. This rare little engine was manufactured in 1948.

(4) Variable Compression by Vernier

Mills Bros Ltd produced some of the best early diesel engines. The rectangular section crankcase Mills 1·3 cc Mk 1 sold in 1947 for £5 5s 6d (£5·27½) including a matched propeller. It was an immediate success on the British market and the author bought one of their first motors from the makers showroom in Southampton Row, Holborn, and saw it run before taking delivery. The model shown in Fig. 60 is the Mk 1 series 2, with the taper finned head. The earliest models had parallel head fins. The example illustrated has been fitted with a Mk 2 venturi as opposed to the straight tube type of the Mk 1 model. It is a good example of how engines are modified in use, as the crankcase, which is serial No. 40 is one of the earliest produced. Power output was $\frac{1}{10}$ bhp at 7000 rpm, and weight 4½ oz. An original Mills Mk 1 series 1, with parallel head fins is shown in Fig. 60A for comparison.

The Mills Mk 2 1·3 cc had a magnesium crankcase (Fig. 61) and this was anodised black in order to stop oxidisation. Both Mk 1 and Mk 2 models were fitted a fuel cut-out as standard. The Mk 2 illustrated is serial No. 36-595.

The Mills ·75 cc was first introduced in rectangular crankcase form, but was soon replaced by the 0·75 Mk 2 in Fig. 62. These were a great favourite especially with scale and sports flyers and remained in production for many years. The serial number of the engine illustrated is 51/992. Both standard and cut-out models were produced, the latter with a cut-out similar to the 1·3 model.

Mills Bros finally produced the 2·4 cc rear rotary induction engine (Fig. 63), which although well made, was rather expensive and lacked a certain edge in performance, by comparison with its competitors. Production figures for this engine were therefore rather low; and the company went on to other work. The serial number of the 2·4 shown is 45/486. The Mills engines, many of which are still in use, are much sought after by flyers and collectors alike.

Fig. 64 shows a Performance Kits Bonnacon fitted with a P75 Mills engine. Propeller is a DC 7-inch × 4-inch. This model is an excellent and very stable sports flyer, featuring mid engine pusher inverted gull-hedral front-plane canard configuration.

The early British Dyne 3 cc was unusual in that it was arranged solely for inverted running. It had a cast-in radial fuel tank. It was a contemporary of the Mills, but made in very small numbers. Dyne also made a 2 cc diesel and a 3·8 cc petrol engine.

George H. Ginns, who was at one time the Chairman of the Coventry & District Model Aircraft club, is now over 80 years old. He is still very active though now retired. From his earliest years he was a keen aeromodeller and before World War 2 he built the 10 cc in-line alternate firing Twin illustrated in Fig. 65. This motor flew a model of 14 ft wing span. During World War 2 he ran the Daimler No 2 shadow factory. In about 1946, he was the works manager of Farmers, a small engineering company in Spon Street, Coventry. George designed the GHG engines, which were put into production. They were well made, solid, long stroke, side port diesels and an early Glow motor.

The Mk 1 2·4 cc was of radial mounted configuration and very few were made (Fig. 66). The 1948 Mk 2 2·4 cc with slot-type compression adjustment was the most prolific. This engine was beam mounted. Each was sold with a Techni-Flo hand-made wooden propeller. Fig. 67 shows the first production batch. In all, 600 of this model were built. Each engine was hand started and test run, before leaving the factory. Only one advertisement was placed as the managing director was anti-advertising, and felt that the engine would sell on its merits.

Other models produced were the GHG 1·5 cc side port diesel, with a total production of 64. There was also a very limited production GHG 4 cc glow engine, shown in Fig. 68. This engine had 360 degree exhaust ports, composed of 17 small holes drilled in the liner, in a similar style to that used for the Yulon 30 engine.

Fig. 10 shows the GHG 4 cc petrol engine, made about 1938. Note the GHG spark plug. This is a fine, well built side port unit, featuring enclosed contact breaker points.

Production of the GHG engines ceased when Mr Ginns left the company for a better position with another firm. The GHG will long be remembered by enthusiasts and modellers as one of the pioneers in British diesel engine production; and the author is pleased to be able to include some of the motors illustrated in his collection.

Grateful acknowledgements are due for the information given by Mr Ginns, without which this section could not have been written.

The Amco (Amco Motors Company of Chester) first produced the ·87 cc

Mk 1 (Fig. 70) which had parallel cylinder fins and a spring loaded cut-out valve. The earlier example illustrated is No. 2769. The numbering on the tops of the cylinder head and needle valve was done to facilitate running settings. The 1948 Mk 2 version had barrel shape cylinder fins. This was followed by the 1949 PB 3·5 (Fig. 71), which was probably the most powerful 3·5 cc diesel of its time, as well as being extremely light in weight. Early versions, like that shown (Serial No. 2798) had a black anodised cylinder head; although subsequent motors were anodised green, and the shaft length reduced (Fig. 72). The author used two of these engines in a twin engine C/L flying wing; which was very fast and spectacular. The PB 3·5 and the later Amco BB 3·5 (ball-bearing), which was designed by Ted Martin, were produced in Alperton, Middlesex. The BB model, fitted with the ball-bearing crankshaft, was very compact and powerful. The cylinder head was usually anodised red. It had rear disc induction with an up-swept air intake, and proved an excellent engine in 1953 for R/C and C/L flying. The power-weight ratio was exceptional.

Frog ('flys right off ground') produced by the old established firm of International Model Aircraft started just after World War 2 with the 1·75 petrol engine (Fig. 73), which sold for £3 in 1948 but was soon abandoned in favour of the Frog 100 1 cc diesel and the 1·6 cc Frog 180. Fig. 74 shows the Mk 2 version of the Frog 100 (serial 14907). The Mk 1 version of this engine had parallel fins similar to the 1·75 petrol motor. All these early Frog engines had reversed threaded prop nuts, and the cylinder heads and complete cylinder assemblies were held to their crankcases by bicycle spoke type studs. Subsequent diesels were the Frog 250 and the Frog 1·49 Vibramatic (Fig. 75). This engine was the first British motor to use a spring loaded clack valve. The cylinder head was red anodised, and the engine illustrated is serial No. 4475. The clack valve was simply a thin shim induction valve retained by a lightly loaded spring. Two of these engines were used in a 41-inch span PK Eclipse Mk 35 C/L stunt model in 1957. The Frog Vibramatic was in fact introduced in 1955. The smallest production Frog engine was the little 50 motor. Fig. 76 shows the early Mk 1 version, originally introduced in 1952. Claimed power output was ·042 bhp at 12,500 rpm. The Mk 2 versions were fitted with Strap type lower crankcases, which accommodated the larger big-end. These motors were also fitted with an elongated fuel tank in about 1955. The Frog 50 was subsequently replaced by the Frog 80 (Fig. 77). An early type Frog 80, serial No. 9869 is illustrated. It had a stylised crankcase, with integral exhaust stacks. The contra-piston incorporated an O seal. A nylon fuel tank was available as an extra in 1957. A glow version, designated the 049 RG was also available and retailed at 49/6 in 1958. This engine weighed 1·9 oz and delivered 0·06 bhp at 1500 rpm.

In 1958 the plain bearing orthodox Frog 150R diesel was introduced developing ·15 bhp at 14,000 rpm, and featuring a blue anodised head. The largest, and most powerful Frog diesels produced were the 2·49 cc BR diesel and 3·49 cc diesel, both of which were intended for C/L stunt work. The latter was also produced with an R/C throttle. Fig. 78 shows the 1·48 cc Frog 1500 Viper. This was a quality engine and employed drum type rear induction

The engine shown has the serial No. 1608, and power output was ·165 bhp at 15,000 rpm. It was produced in relatively small numbers, and was probably the best Frog engine ever made. The crankcase is a high-class vapour blasted die-casting with cooling fins on the under side. The shaft ran in two ball races. The cylinder head is turned from highly polished aluminium. Steel parts are blued and a friction type needle valve is fitted. The cylinder head is fitted with an Armstrong HELI-Coil high tensile compression screw friction insert. Each engine was hand started before despatch. After the production of the Viper engine in 1961, and the inexpensive Venom glow version which looked similar, but utilised a plain bearing crankshaft, Frog engines ceased to be manufactured by IMA (International Model Aircraft) and were latterly produced by Davies-Charlton in the Isle of Man. A few parts were interchangeable with engines in the DC range, such as the DC Spitfire, Sabre and Wasp ·049 cubic inch. The Wasp glow was also marketed as the Frog Venom ·049 in radial tank form. The Frog versions were given a red anodised cylinder head. In about 1974 the Frog range disappeared from the market.

In 1949 the light 4½ oz 3·5 cc Weston Stunt Special was introduced specially for stunt C/L flying. Both this motor and the Weston 3 cc diesel were made in small numbers in Weston-super-Mare. The 3 cc was made in 1948. Out of a total production of 26 Weston stunt engines, six were of the original 3·5 cc side port layout, and the remaining 20 were front rotary shaft valve stunt specials. In the same year MS in Newcastle introduced a very interesting 1·24 cc front induction side port with a clear tank formed around the crankshaft, weight 2⅞ oz. This motor was radially mounted and sold for £4 15s 6d. (£4·77½). This front induction side port layout was also used by the 1945 American Melcraft Blue Streak petrol engine and the Zeiss Jena 1 cc.

The rare and nicely proportioned and constructed French 3·5 cc side port Boss Moran, was in production in 1947. Very few of these delightful motors were made. The same firm also made a 5 cc diesel. The Boss Moran was designed as a general purpose motor for the F/F or early C/L models of the period.

The K Engineering Co. of Gravesend in Kent were very prolific engine manufacturers. Harry Kemp started with the 4·4 cc side port diesel, which was also made, in small numbers, as an 8·8 cc in-line twin. The 4·4 cc model was always finished in black. The specimen illustrated in Fig. 79 has serial No. 522, and was produced in 1947. All K engines can be easily identified by the fact that they have an encircled letter K cast into the crankcase. Then came the 1 cc K Eagle (Fig. 80), which was subsequently produced in series 2 form with FRV induction, and the rare K 1·9 (Fig. 81). This motor (serial No. 762) had a very small diameter FRV air intake, and the needle valve incorporated a most unusual friction mechanism comprising a spring, resembling half a safety pin with one arm located in the front shaft housing and the other arm impinging, via a slot, directly on the needle. The large prop nut was made from magnesium. In 1948 came the much sought after little Kemp Hawk ·2 cc (Fig. 82). The engine illustrated is serial No. 1601. The first ones had three webs on the shaft housing, and a metal tank, but these were soon replaced with the four webbed plastic tank model illustrated. In 1949 a Mk 2 version was introduced, which, although still of 0·2 cc, was of completely different design, using FRV induction. The final offering, known as the Hawk Special was derived from the FRV layout, but the air intake was moved from the top to the bottom of the shaft housing and a large radial mounting back-plate was incorporated. In 1949 the K Kestrel was introduced as an inexpensive diesel of 1·9 cc (Fig. 83), which was much favoured by C/L stunt flyers. The motor illustrated is serial No. K449. The K Falcon 2 cc (Fig. 84) was a much more carefully built version of the Kestrel. It is a much rarer engine than the Kestrel, and can be identified by the fact that the cylinder fins continue below the exhaust ports. The largest model in the K range was the K Vulture, and three versions were made; all were 5 cc FRV diesels. The Mk 1 (Fig. 85) had fins on the top of the cylinder head, but not below the exhaust ports. Mk 1 Vulture, serial No. 126, is illustrated in Fig. 85. The Mk 2 was finned all the way to the Dog Collar, which held the cylinder barrel to the crankcase. This Dog Collar was a design feature of all Kestrel, Falcon and Vulture engines. The Mk 3 Vulture (Fig. 86) looked like the Mk 2, but had a plain cylinder head. This model is often referred to by collectors as the Bald Headed Vulture. It also had radial mounting lugs and an angled venturi insert. This motor was produced in 1949, and the motor illustrated is serial No. 3009. Power output for the Vulture series was increased as production progressed. The final engine to be produced by the K engineering company was the inexpensive K Tornado, of 1·9 cc, which was a glow engine derivative of the Kestrel marketed in 1950.

 Electronic Developments (Surrey) Ltd were the largest producers of diesel engines in England for many years. Their factory at Island Farm Road, West Molesey, Surrey, was large and well equipped with such items as centreless grinders and fully automatic lathes, which in general were not used by other contemporary manufacturers in England at this time, either for reasons of finance or due to lower production. After the ED Mk 2 (Fig. 57) mentioned earlier, came the ED Competition Special (Fig. 87), which was a very popular motor and in production for many years. The motor shown is serial No. K141-9C, and features the relatively rare plunger type cut-out valve. The ED Bee 1 cc Mk 1 (Fig. 88) and subsequent later Bee models were the biggest selling ED engines. Price was very low. The date of manufacture can easily be ascertained from the serial number. The motor in Fig. 88 is No. IF 617 51. The last two digits indicate that this engine's date is 1951. Following production motors were the ED 2·49 Mk 3 side port with separate hang tank and the ED 3·46. The smallest motor in the range, with a bore of ·312 inch and stroke of ·375 inch was the ED Baby ·46 cc. which weighed 1·4 oz and developed ·04 bhp at 12,000 rpm. The motor illustrated in Fig. 89 is, in fact, the Mk 2 version of the Baby engine, and is serial numbered DF 55 32. The Mk 1 version of the Baby, introduced in 1952, had round exhaust ports, as opposed to the slot type ports of the Mk 2 version illustrated.

 It is interesting to note that the author used an ED Baby Mk 2 to obtain the British Lightweight tailless power model record on July 27, 1954, on

Epsom Downs with an Ionosphere Mk 13A model. This record still stood in 1975, twenty-one years later!

Fig. 90 shows the prototype ED Hunter engine used to fly the Radio Queen across the Channel. This prototype is devoid of serial numbers, and is an extremely well made unit. The engine is of 3·46 cc capacity, and the production version developed ·265 bhp at 10,000 rpm. All-up weight was $7\frac{3}{4}$ oz and the crankshaft was ball-bearing mounted. Bore and stroke were ·656 inch and ·625 inch respectively. The cross Channel flight was unique in that it was the first time that a R/C model had done this feat, and was a considerable achievement. ED R/C gear was used.

The ED Racer 2·46 cc twin ball race rear disc-induction motor was a very reliable and powerful unit, which remained in production for many years. The induction disc on the early Racers was of alloy; but as performance was increased for competitive events, this tended to fracture and so a Tufnol fibre disc was substituted. In standard form the Mk 2 Racer produced ·26 bhp at 14,000 rpm. The last model racers had a front crankcase housing similar to the ED Super Fury. The first production Racers lack the webs between the front and rear crankshaft ball race housings. The Mk 2 version is shown in Fig. 91. These engines can be dated by reference to their serial numbers. Thus the example shown which is serial No. RM 130 51 was produced in 1951. The crankcases of these engines were cast in Magnesium alloy and were anodised black. The cylinder fins, prop driver and spinner nut of the Mk 2 Racer illustrated are anodised red. The Racer and the Hunter were in simultaneous production for several years. Early Hunters had fins on the cylinder head and a long crankshaft illustrated in Fig. 90, while later models had a flat anodised cylinder head. The ED Hornet 1·46 was an inexpensive rear rotary disc-induction sports motor and the ED Fury 1·49 cc a smaller version of the Racer, complete with twin ball race crankshaft. The later Super Fury, Fig. 92, had a side mounted ratchet needle valve assembly instead of the earlier upright coil friction type. Power was boosted from ·13 bhp at 14,000 rpm for the Fury to a creditable ·185 bhp at 17,000 rpm for the Super Fury. The Super Fury found considerable favour with $\frac{1}{2}$A team racing enthusiasts.

Perhaps the best known of all the ED engines is the rotary disc-induction Bee. It was made for many years in several versions. Fig. 88 shows the 1951 Mk 1, with three bolts holding the head down; and Fig. 93 a 1957 Mk 2 fitted in a Performance Kits Apex. Over 300,000 ED Bees were sold, a very high production figure for a British engine. B. Miles, the ED designer produced a very powerful 5 cc BR diesel in 1952, which ED subsequently sold as the ED Special. It was used for early stunt and R/C models such as the negative stagger Climax biplanes and Eclipse stunt C/L models. It produced ·5 bhp at 12,000 rpm and weighed $9\frac{1}{2}$ oz. The production Miles special engine is illustrated in Fig. 94. The 1960 ED Pep (Fig. 95), an inexpensive front rotary shaft induction motor, sold for £1 18s 4d (£1·91$\frac{1}{2}$) including metal tank. Weight was only $1\frac{3}{4}$ oz. The crankcase was pressure die-cast from LN2 light alloy. The piston was made from Meehanite and the con-rod from Hiduminium. The crankshaft and cylinder were of hardened steel and the main bearing was fitted with a bronze bush. This little engine, with the capacity of ·8 cc represented exceptional value but, by ED standards, relatively few were made. After the fire, which severely damaged the ED factory, the last ED engines to be made were the loop scavenged side port ED Cadet 1 cc, based on the Bee, and selling for £1 18s 4d (£1·91½) which was the first diesel to be sold complete with a silencer; and the Hawk 1·5 cc front rotary, which was made in West Germany under licence, and bore a strong resemblance to the Webra 1·5. Many of the ED Cadets had to be returned as faulty, due to poor compression seal, and shortly afterwards ED ceased production; although some parts were taken on by a separate company in Surbiton and production of some models continued in modified form.

After the demise of the original ED company the ED Pep crankcases were taken over by De-Za-Lux Developments Ltd, a company in Brentford, Middlesex, who produced the De-Za-Lux Za92 in 1963. This engine, also distributed by Performance Kits, was very similar to the original Pep. Production ceased as the crankcases expired. It was a good little sports engine and very inexpensive, with a retail price of £2 9s 0d (£2·45) in 1964.

The original ME engines were produced by Marown Engineering company in the Isle of Man. There was the 1 cc Heron and the 1·5 cc Snipe. Production was subsequently taken over by Moore Engineering Ltd, and the Heron and Snipe motors were reintroduced with minor modifications. Both engines have integrally cast exhaust stubs and are available with a pair of neat exhaust silencers as an extra. Early models had red anodised cylinder heads, while later ones had a polished aluminium head. Fig. 96 shows a 1975 ME Heron ·97 cc motor. The Moore Engineering produced Snipe engines have a separate turned venturi intake as opposed to the earlier Marown manufactured cast ones, which were formed in unit with the crankcase.

The American O. K. Herkimer and McCoy companies produced ·049 cubic inch diesel engines. Fig. 97 shows the McCoy version, which incorporated a plastic O-ring as a compression seal. This looks like a plastic contra-piston ring. The engine featured is radially mounted via the cover plate retaining bolts and has a red anodised cylinder head. Duro-Glo is inscribed on the crankcase, indicating the engine's glo-plug ancestry.

The Elfin engines were produced by Aerol Engineering Co., Henry Street, Liverpool, the makers of the first high performance radially ported diesels. These were the famous Aerol Gremlin Mk 6, 2 cc engines, which were almost immediately replaced by the much better known Elfin 1·8 cc. Using the Arden porting system, the Elfin 1·8 (Fig. 98) was the perfect F/F and C/L engine and won many competitions in 1949. Fig. 99 shows the F/F version with a hole in its radial mount to accommodate its plastic tank. Compare this with Fig. 98, which is basically a C/L model with a solid radial mount. There was also a 2·49 cc version shown in Fig. 100, which was powerful, well made, and highly thought of. The second generation Elfins were plain bearing beam mount engines of 1·49 cc and 2·49 cc. The latter motor is shown in Fig. 101. The 1·49 motor was introduced in 1950 and in 1952 won the International Power championships. Power output was ·15 bhp at 13,500 rpm. All Elfins were powerful, compact, and light. In 1952 the delightful small radially mounted Elfin 50 ·5 cc F/F motor was introduced, which bore a certain similarity in appearance to the earlier 1·8 engines, but had the fuel tank mounted underneath the crankcase. The third generation Elfins, introduced in 1954, were all of the clack valve type. There was a 1·49 BR, 1·8 BR and 2·49 BR. They all incorporated a barrel type crankcase and twin BR crankshafts. The author used two of these 1·49 BRs in a record-breaking (RAF MAA) Ionosphere Mk 16 tandem double delta flying wing. Fig. 102 shows the last of the Elfins, the 2·49 BR. This was in production from 1955–8 and gave ·23 bhp at 13,300 rpm.

The much later Taifun Hurrikan 1·5 cc, from Germany, used a similar clack valve induction system. This engine is illustrated in Fig. 103. The air intake is covered with a gauze filter and the motor features a twin BR crankshaft and red anodised cylinder head.

Davies-Charlton started production with the DC Wildcat. The 1947 Mk 1 was radially mounted. The Mk 2 of 1948 had beam mounts and Fig. 104 shows the 1949 Mk 3 model, which gave ·34 bhp at 10,000 rpm. It was very similar to the Mk 2, but had improved porting and a lighter piston. It was a well-made, though heavy, 5 cc diesel, featuring a knurled needle locking disc and air bleed fuel cut-out. This motor was superseded by the DC 350 in 1950 and DC 350 Mk 2 (Fig. 105). The early DC 350 model only had three head retaining screws, and a one-piece compression lever, while the Mk 2 version illustrated (serial No. 4347) had six head retaining bolts and a V-type compression vernier. These were excellent high power type sports engines ideal for early R/C and C/L models. The author used one of them for national and international R/C competitions in the Meson Mk 2 in 1952. This was a low-wing model, featuring three tail fins. The engines were reliable, which is more than can be said for the R/C gear, used in the same machines, which incorporated 3Q4 acorn type hard valve sets and vibrating relays. A glo-plug version of the DC 350 Mk 2 was introduced, and this, illustrated in Fig. 106, is a late model glo engine serial No. 1915. At this point DC amalgamated with Allbon engines, who had been producing the Allbon 2·8 cc side-port (made in Cople, Bedfordshire), Allbon Spitfire FRV, and in 1950 the Allbon Javelin 1·5 cc FRV and Allbon Dart Mk 1, ·5 cc and they all moved to the Isle of Man. DC dropped the Wildcat, but the DC 350 was modified and appeared as the Manxman (Fig. 107) with red anodised head in 1956. They also produced the Bambi of ·2 cc in 1954 and the Mk 1 Rapier 2·5 cc rear disc induction twin BR diesel (Fig. 108) which had a green anodised cylinder head. The early Allbon Javelin and Dart were replaced with DC versions and in 1953 the Allbon Spitfire was added to the range. The name Allbon gradually disappeared from the crankcases, and was no longer used as the motors were modified, although the capacities still remained 1·5 cc, ·5 cc, and 1 cc, for the three motors mentioned above and ·2 cc for the Bambi, which was the smallest motor ever to be made by DC. The 1953 DC Dart Mk 2 had a red anodised head, whereas the Mk 1 Allbon model was always green. The very popular DC Merlin ·75, was released in 1954, together with the Super Merlin, which was a derivative featuring a red anodised head and spinner nut together with a fitted tank. In 1955 the DC Sabre 1·49 cc replaced the Javelin. In July 1973 the Mk 2 Rapier was introduced, fitted with a silencer as standard, and with other small modifications. Earlier Rapiers had a green cylinder head and rather superior brass cap compression bar ends, whereas the Mk 2 versions always had a blue anodised cylinder head. In 1959 the Quick-start spring and cam were introduced. Other very popular DC engines were the Bantam and much later the Wasp ·049 glo motors. Mr Davies also made an eccentric compression diesel, but this was only a prototype.

Allan Allbon left DC and started again in Milton, Berkshire, in 1959; when in company with Mr Saunders he made the excellent small A-S55 ·55 cc FRV diesel, which was one of the best ·5 cc engines ever made in series production. In 1964 the A-S55 sold for £2 11s 0d (£2·55). Weight was 1½ oz. The engine featured a forged con-rod in RR56 alloy. Maximum power was ·052 bhp at 12,000 rpm. After a considerable number of these engines had been produced, Mr Allbon went into the optical industry.

In 1959 the Busek ·1 cc baby high performance rear rotary diesel was produced in small numbers in Czechoslovakia by Gustave Busek. Performance was far above other diesels, such as the Bambi and the Dragonfly, of comparable capacity.

Majesco Motors from Parkstone in Dorset, who produced the 4·5 cc side port petrol engine (Fig. 25) made a considerable number of 2·2 cc side port diesels using the same lower crankcase casting as the petrol motor. These motors were also fitted with twin exhaust stubs. Their weak point was their rather delicate beam mounting lugs; they were reliable in all other respects.

Reeves of Shifnal in Salop, made the 6 cc petrol motor at about the same time as the Majesco 4·5 cc, just after World War 2. They then made the Reeves 3·5 cc FRV diesel, which the author used in a 5-foot span F/F sports model as well as the Eclipse Mk 2 stunter, which flew well in 1948. The Reeves Goblin 2·5 cc was also used to power a three engined helicopter. The Goblin was a compact rear rotary induction diesel with integral casting exhaust stacks. This motor was in production in 1962. The range was completed with the Reeves H18 which was a 1·8 cc rear disc induction sports diesel, which in common with an Elfin 1·49 BR was used to power the Meson Mk 6 46-inch span F/F model in 1954. Plans for this model appeared in the *Model Aircraft* magazine in March 1955.

Like many early English model diesels, Reeves concentrated on piston bore fits, and general internal finish, often at the expense of external finish. The Reeves 3·5 cc is a perfect example of this philosophy. In 1948 Reeves advertised the 3·5, and claimed that every one of these engines would hold its compression seal for a minimum period of one hour; and should this not be the case the engine could be retained free of charge! The engine purchased by the author from the factory, proved this claim to be correct.

There were a large number of small production engines in the late 1940s and throughout the 1950s. Many were well made, but were mainly locally distributed, such as the Foursome 1·2 cc side port from Brighton. All up weight, including prop was only 5 oz; but due to its large crankcase volume and consequent low volumetric efficiency, power was below that of the currently popular Mills 1·3 Mk 2, and very considerably down on the Elfin 1·8, which was in production at the same time. The 1947 HP Mk 3 Series 2 from Barnet, was made in very small numbers, and used a similar lower crankcase and carburettor assembly to the HP Mk 2 petrol engine. The tank was always of black plastic. Fig. 109 shows one of the rare HP Mk 3 4 cc diesels with the serial No. D-218. It would turn a 12-inch propeller at 7000 rpm. The series 1 had 4 long studs to retain the head. The 1948 BMP 3·5 (Fig. 202) which was one of the first English diesels to use a ball race crankshaft always had the multiple random drillings in the massive beam engine mount to reduce weight. BMP, which stands for Bijou Mechanical Productions (Bournemouth) Ltd also produced a radially mounted small twin BR ·9 cc diesel. Both engines were made in Bournemouth and sold via J. Kenworthy in the Charminster Road. Early BMP 3·5 diesels were devoid of serial numbers. The Ace ·5 cc, from London, was a nice little SP sports motor, with a crankcase machined from solid, which was in production at the same time as the Amco ·87 Mk 1; as was the very light 1½ oz 1948, MEC Mk 4 1·2 cc side port diesel, which was radially mounted.

The Comet Mk 1 (Fig. 110) was marketed in 1948. It sold at the very low price of £2 15s 0d (£2·75). There was also a Mk 2 version; but total production was very small. Both versions had a capacity of ·4 cc.

In 1961 Dydesdyne Ltd of Slough produced a few Dynamic ·049 diesels. This was an attempt to produce a very high performance competition diesel engine for ·049 F/F events. The competition model had a twin ball race crankshaft. A less expensive plane bearing ·049 model was also produced for sports flying. These motors were only sold direct to the public and to model shops, and were never distributed through engine wholesalers.

The Aquilio Baby 1 cc and the Alag X3 2·5 cc engines from Hungary were imported into England for a time from 1956. Both were FRV sports type engines, with plain bearings. The Alag X3 was unusual in that it had a red plastic rear cover plate and venturi inserts. This engine was used as an inexpensive C/L stunt sports motor, and was used by beginners in such models as the PK Proton combat flying wing and the PK Lynx negative stagger C/L stunt bi-plane. There was also an Alag ·25 cc FRV diesel, which featured a gold anodised cylinder head. Fits on this engine were below standard.

The Clansman 5 cc was a well built early front rotary shaft induction motor with up-draught carburettor. These engines were produced by the Caledonia Model Co. of Pipps Street, Glasgow, which was an old established model shop.

Eta Instruments of Watford produced the first quality English 5 cc diesel (Fig. 111) and was still producing engines in 1974; although in recent years they have specialised in team race and FAI class F/F engines, such as the 2·5 cc Eta Elite. The motor illustrated in Fig. 111 is serial No. 44894, and has a matt grey finish. These engines were fitted with a lever operated choke valve and spring-loaded cut-out. The large exhaust stacks are detachable, and the

Eta emblem, in the form of the Greek letter Eta is featured on the front transfer port cover, above a No 5, denoting its 5 cc capacity. Eta production ceased in 1975.

In Italy the early Super Elia SP 5 cc and long stroke Alfa Mk 1 were in production at the same time as the Eta 5 cc diesel; together with such interesting engines as the well made Atomatic 4·4 cc, which had a fixed jet, a fuel tank surrounding the crankshaft and variable air flow via a valve operated by a lever mounted above the crankshaft. The author used one of these Atomatic 4·4 cc diesels for an early C/L flying wing type model, known as the Platter, with great success in 1948. Atomatic also produced a scaled down version of the engine, which was reduced to 1 cc.

Fig. 112 shows the Italian Osam diesel. The same basic crankcase was used for both petrol and diesel versions. It will be noted that the front shaft housing is machined ready for the petrol version's contact breaker assembly. The engine illustrated is serial No. 60873. This engine bears a strong resemblance to early Super Tigre motors. Later Super Tigre engines, which were systematically developed from the early versions mentioned above, can be seen by reference to Fig. 113, which features the Super Tigre G.32, a lovely little 1 cc ball race diesel, with rear drum induction. The crankcase is vapour blasted, and head red anodised. The end of the drum valve bearing is protected with a rubber dust sealer. Fig. 114 shows the larger G.30 plain bearing version of the same motor. There are a vast number of Super Tigre engines and they are still being built today.

From Oslo in Norway came the beautifully made David-Andersen engines. Fig. 115 shows an early Drabant Mk 1 2·5 cc model, as imported into England by Performance Kits in 1960 and used one year in the Gold Trophy in an Eclipse Mk 46 C/L stunt model. Fig. 116 features the very last Drabant 2·5 cc Mk 2, duly signed by its makers and dated 1972. Other D-A engines included the D-A Satellitt 1 cc, which developed ·1 bhp at 12,000 rpm. Fig. 117 shows one of these engines mounted in a PK Orbit-Sports intermediate C/L stunt kit. The D-A Tellus is a plain bearing FRV 2·5 cc sports engine, bearing a strong resemblance to the Drabant. All the above mentioned D-A engines were built to very high engineering standards. Nice detail features are the compression screw friction device, featuring a split tapered collet, and the needle valve variable friction mechanism which can be adjusted with a nut on the tapered spray-bar extension.

From Amsterdam, in Holland came the Veenhoven R-250 BR 2·47 cc, known as the Typhoon R-250. Power rate ratio was very good with an output of ·33 bhp at 14,200 rpm and a weight of 4·7 oz. Fig. 118 shows an example of this model, serial No. 38. The prop driver was located with two Allen keys and the cylinder head is anodised red. The same firm produced the Typhoon 5 cc BR diesel (Fig. 119) and the interesting in-line 7 cc ball race twin, described later. The range was made up with a 2·47 cc plain bearing version of the R-250, the Typhoon Mk 4 4·5 cc glow motor and finally the Super-Typhoon 10 cc twin ball race racing engine. Typhoon engines were imported and distributed by Performance Kits in December 1959. A speed of 237 kph was reached at Schiphol aerodrome with a Super-Typhoon motor. Another rare Dutch engine is the 2·47 cc Favoriet, manufactured by Thuella Motors. It features a rotating rear cover plate, which in the vertical position allows for beam-mounting, and when set horizontally is intended as a radial mount. The motor features rear induction, through this mounting plate. Maximum bhp was ·26 at 13,000 rpm.

Czechoslovakia has always been strong on diesel engine production. In 1946 they produced the Atom 1·8 cc side port and Super Atom 1·8 cc. The Super Atom followed in 1947. The Super Atom had a side mounted intake tube, which featured a fuel feed from a tank, which was concentric with the crankshaft, as opposed to the neat rear mounted tank of the standard 1·8 model. A larger version, known as the Atom Major, featuring a transparent tank bowl, and of 3·5 cc capacity was also available in 1947. All these early Atom engines featured three point radial mounting lugs and polished spinner nuts. Liners were located by the threaded cylinder heads. Some relatively recent engines are the plain bearing FRV Atom 1A (Fig. 120), and featuring a gold anodised cylinder head, back-plate and spinner nut.

Fig. 121 shows one of the latest MVVS 1·5 cc diesels from the Czech State Model Institute. Serial numbers of the engines illustrated in Figs 120 and 121 are 0319 and 213 respectively. The MVVS is one of a large range of engines, mostly designed for international competition purposes, and is of excellent workmanship throughout. Fig. 123 illustrates the Pfeffer ·6 cc, which was manufactured in 1975. Mr Pfeffer was formerly with the Letna engine company. The Pfeffer is a most interesting and well made unit. It features a square section anodised cylinder head, triangular radial mounting, surface jet side port induction and twin exhaust stacks. A locking bar for the compression lever is also provided, and this, together with the compression lever and front housing retaining screws are neatly blued. Another new motor, introduced in 1975, is the OTM Kolibri ·8 cc (Fig. 124). Cylinder head and prop driver/spinner nut are anodised black. The motor is supplied with a multi-tool to aid maintenance and repair.

The Motop Mk 16 is an excellent 2·5 cc rear disc induction engine from Russia. It is ultra-smooth running, with a carefully counter-balanced twin BR crankshaft. Fig. 125 shows one of these motors with serial No. 72-1005. The motor is exceptionally well finished with red anodised scalloped head and driver/spinner nut. Fuel feed is effected via a banjo union. Fig. 126 shows a Russian Vertorek ·5 cc and Fig. 127 a Rhythm 2·5 cc drum induction motor with the serial No. 696. Rhythm is the English translation of the Russian Ritm. The motor comes from the Dosaae factory in Kiev.

In 1975 Australian diesel engines were still in production by the old established firm of Gordon Burford & Co. Pty Ltd. These motors made in NSW have been distributed in England by Performance Kits since 1968. Fig. 128 shows one of the first model Taipan (the name of an Australian poisonous snake) 1·5 cc diesels. This engine featured combined beam and radial mounting, and is shown mounted in a PK Apex kit. Earlier engines from this manufacturer were called Sabre and glow versions Glow-Chief; but both these names have now been dropped. The last production Taipan diesel was the very powerful twin BR 2·5 cc FRV, designed for FAI events. This engine was phased out early in 1975.

With the advent of competition Combat C/L flying, A. E. Rivers Ltd of Hounslow, Middlesex, who were sub-contractors to Fairey Aviation, produced in 1960 the 2·49 cc Silver Streak and 3·49 cc Silver Arrow, which with over ·4 bhp was the most powerful 3·5 cc diesel in the world. A variable speed control unit was available, as an extra, to fit the tapping in the rear crankcase cover. This worked as a crankcase pressure bleed and was intended for R/C and C/L scale models. The tapping could also be fitted with a special nipple for the pressurisation of C/L model fuel tanks. Both Rivers models used a unique taper roller needle bearing crankshaft assembly. Fig. 129 shows a Rivers Silver Arrow. These engines seriously challenged the established Oliver Tiger 2·5 cc and Oliver Major which were the standard engines for competitive combat events. The Silver Streak was also available, at extra cost, as a specially tuned model for competition flying, and retailed at £7 15s 0d (£7·75).

The excellent Oliver Tiger 2·5 cc BR FRV is still in production. The author used one of the first sand-cast 2·5 cc BR motors to set the British National Open power driven tailless record on Epsom Downs on March 21, 1954, and this record still stands! Early Oliver Tiger engines were made in very small numbers, and the first aircraft versions were developed from successful model race car units. Mrs Oliver used to run a small news sheet entitled Tiger Tails which was circulated to Oliver Tiger owners, keeping them up to date with technical developments and advising them of competition successes. Later motors were the Oliver Cub 1·5 cc and Oliver Major 3·5 cc. A prototype in-line alternate firing twin was also made, but never went into production.

Fig. 130 shows an example of the 1974 Zom 2·5 cc twin BR diesel, which is produced in Madrid, Spain. The motor illustrated is serial No. D1294, and this engine bears a certain similarity to the English motors mentioned above.

J. E. Ballard, who was a director of Electronic Developments Ltd, left that company and produced the JB (John Ballard) Bomb 1 cc and JB Atom 1·5 cc in 1957. Fig. 131 shows one of these latter units in a PK Apex, which was fitted with single channel R/C. Power was low, due to low volumetric efficiency, but external finish was good.

In America the Deezil (Fig. 132) was in production. Quality was poor, but price very low. There were also a few Bunch and Vivell diesels, with the compression adjusted with an Allen key. The Vivell had a unique feature in that its contra-piston fitted into its cylinder head as opposed to the top of the liner. This engine was similar in appearance to the fixed compression model shown in Fig. 53.

The Embee, whose name was derived from M for Moore and B for Bailey was originally produced in a factory in Rookery Lane, Groby, Leicester, in 1968. The Embee ·75 Mk 1 (Fig. 133) was the only engine produced, before the factory reverted to production of machines for fabric manufacture. In 1969 Mr Moore left the partnership and produced the engines from his own premises in Fairfax Road, Leicester, trading as P & M Engineering

His products also included the EmBee ·75 Mk 2 and Mk 3, and the flat geared twin. Fig. 134 shows an EmBee 10 1 cc fitted to a scaled down version of the 1938 Cloud Airmaster. Other motors were the ·75 BR and ·75 Mk 4. This latter engine had a single cylinder fin and was made in 1971. It is illustrated in Fig. 135. The flat twin is shown in Fig. 136. The final production EmBee model was the 2·5 cc diesel. Very few of these were made.

The Jena, made by the Zeiss Camera Co. in East Germany, was available in three versions, all with ball race shafts. Fig. 137 shows the 1 cc front induction side port. Fig. 138 shows the blue headed 2 cc rear rotary induction motor and Fig. 139 the 2·5 cc black headed unit, in this case, fitted with an R/C carburettor. All motors have compression locking bars, and the 1 cc is also equipped with a coil starter spring.

In Western Germany the Taifun range is much respected. Fig. 140 shows a Hobby Mk 1 1 cc FRV, as fitted in an asymetric F/F flying wing of three foot span (the X-AD-3), while the Mk 2 version of the Hobby is shown in Fig. 141. The 2·5 cc Rasant II, often called the Tea Pot Spout model, named for obvious reasons, is shown in Fig. 142. Serial numbers of the motors in Figs 141 and 142 are 35131 and 10119 respectively. Taifun also produced the Hurrikan 1·5 cc clack-valve motor, previously mentioned, and illustrated in Fig. 103. Later production Taifun engines were the Orkan and Zyklon of 2·47 cc and the 3·5 cc Bison. All are good soundly engineered motors. The Zyklon being specifically intended for R/C use.

Micron of Paris, the makers of the earlier mentioned fixed compression 5 cc diesels, are the oldest firm still producing diesels in continuous production. Earlier engines were designed by M. Gladieux and later ones by G. Maraget, who produced the excellent Meteore-Maraget ·9 cc side-port in 1946. Fig. 143 shows the Micron Meteor ·9 cc diesel. All Micron engines are produced to the very highest engineering standards, and are built with integrity. The little Meteor shown features the typical Micron needle-valve assembly which is made up from six parts, and gives a smooth yet vibration-free adjustment. The needle is threaded internally, and locked, with a steel nut, to its brass locating slipper. This slipper has four slots cut in it, and is tensioned with a coil spring over the slotted end. The 1946 Micron 2·5 cc side port has long since been replaced by the modern 2·5 cc FRV BR models, such as the 2·5 cc racing unit shown in Fig. 144. It will be noted that the same design of needle valve assembly is incorporated on this 1975 model.

When Amco and JB ceased production, Denis Allen, who had been associated with the production of both these engines in their latter stages at Alperton, went on to produce the A-M (Allen-Mercury) diesels in conjunction with Mercury Kits. Models were A-M 10 (1 cc), A-M 15 (1·5 cc), A-M 25 (2·5 cc) and A-M 35 (3·5 cc). All were plain bearing, simple FRV motors, the 35 being a bored version of the 25 and the 15 being a bored version of the 10. The 10 and 15 can be identified by their respective green and blue anodised heads. The 25 and 35 were anodised black and pink respectively. Fig. 145 shows a Mk 1 version of the A-M 25. These early A-M 25s featured inset head retaining bolts. The motor shown is serial No. 1437. The later Mk 2 versions of both 25 and 35 engines had their heads retained by four long bolts, which entered the top of the cylinder head, and went through into the crankcase lugs. All A-M motors had good power/weight ratios, and the author used one of these engines to win the All Britain Rally at the old Handley Page aerodrome at Radlett in Hertfordshire, on September 16, 1956, flying an Ionosphere Mk 14.

Probably the last 5 cc diesel to remain in production was the lovely Polish Super Sokol (Sokol: Kestrel in Polish) BR stunt engine, featuring rear disc-induction (Fig. 146). The cylinder head is anodised black with spinner-nut and prop driver finished in red. Workmanship is of a high order. This type of engine finally gave way to the ·35 cubic inch glow engine for stunt C/L work, mainly due to the latter's lighter weight, greater flexibility, simpler starting, and above all lower price.

In August 1974 the Apex Nipper ·375 cc rear rotary induction motor (Fig. 147), designed by Mr Les Saxby, was produced in small quantities. This excellent little engine is capable of turning a 5-inch × 3-inch propeller at 11,000 rpm. Fig. 148 shows the Saxby designed and built ·375 cc and ·5 cc diesels; both engines were specially designed for small F/F scale and sports models.

At the time of writing it is hoped that an improved version of the Apex Nipper may go into production by Performance Kits, and prototypes are currently under test. These motors are known as the X-Ult ·375. Early engines have crankcases entirely machined from the solid. Construction and finish are to the highest standard. Care has been taken to keep the overall length as short as possible, and the engines have exceptionally good torque characteristics enabling them to swing a relatively large diameter propeller. All mating surfaces have surface machined joints, and no gaskets are employed.

Mr Ben Buckle of Aero Designs, Farringdon, has been working on a simplified version of this motor, featuring front rotary induction and three head retaining bolts. The general appearance of the prototype is rather similar to a miniature PAW 1·49. A few were made in 1975.

There were of course a vast number of ultra-low production units made by model engineers throughout the world. Sometimes they were built from casting kits, such as the 1948 Masco Buzzard 2·8 cc side port and sometimes machined from solid bar stock as with the clack-valve Fisher 3·5 (Fig. 149), made in Princess Gate, London, and the fine little Dragonfly ·1 cc, which was sold complete with an alloy propeller. In France the Morin range of engines were sold as casting kits, and included a vast fixed-compression diesel, with over-sized head fins.

Raylite of Nottingham, who were a retail model shop, marketed the Rapier 1 cc in 1948. The same firm also sold the Raylite Panther, which was made by Oliver, and was a forerunner of the Oliver Tiger. In 1948–9, the very old-established Hallam Company of Poole in Dorset, introduced a 2·5 cc diesel, but very few were in fact produced.

(5) Variable Compression by Moving Liner

Between 1947–8, the Speed Demon 30, which is illustrated in Fig. 150, was manufactured on Long Island, New York. The greater part of the motor is machined from bar stock, and bears the serial No. 135 5. On test, this actual motor turned a 10-inch diameter × 6-inch pitch propeller at 6,400 rpm and a 14-inch × 6-inch at 3,600 rpm. In operation, the motor ran smoothly, although it was important to remember that compression was increased by rotating the compression lever anti-clockwise instead of the usual clockwise direction, as is the case with all other diesels. It is thought that about 2000 to 3000 of these engines were made, and some of them were fitted with turned spinner nuts, instead of the standard hex-nut fitted to the motor illustrated. When the compression is altered the blind bored liner is moved linearly inside the cylinder, and this also has the effect of altering the porting. With a high-speed motor, this would be a great disadvantage, but the Speed Demon, in spite of its name, has a relatively low performance, even for its year of manufacture, and the system works remarkably well. It is interesting to note that the engine's capacity is actually ·27 cubic inch, although some of them were in fact ·29 cubic inch, which gave rise to the 30 in the nomenclature.

5 : Multi-Cylinder Engines

(1) Petrol

MULTI-CYLINDER engines are of special interest, both as a result of their greater mechanical complexity and their relative rarity and exclusivity—due to high intial cost, lengthy development and subsequent small production.

The excellent 20 cc OK Herkimer SP flat twin was one of those made, in relatively large numbers, starting before World War 1 by the Herkimer Tool & Model Works Inc. of New York. The new example in Fig. 151 is a 1946 specimen, No. 60941. This engine would swing a 20-inch × 6-inch hydulignum propeller and it was important to keep the revs down to avoid fracture of the welded crankshaft. This motor was used for early R/C models. Half a bhp was claimed at 5,600 rpm. Weight is 22 oz. The crankcase is split down the centre line. Con-rods were made in one piece. Due to its smooth running characteristics, it was one of the first engines to be recommended for R/C. Low vibration was very important with these early R/C models, where the rudder servo was operated through the medium of a sensitive electro-mechanical relay.

The Wasp Twin, from Micro Models of Van Nuys California was a ·6 cubic inch motor. Fig. 152 shows the early black crackle finish six-screw model (serial No. 3263), which developed $\frac{1}{2}$ bhp at 10,000 rpm. Later versions had ten screws holding the crankcase halves together. Fits, however, on this early model are very good. The ten-screw Wasp engines were known as the Wasp Special when supplied with black crackle finish, and as Scout Twins if painted flame colour. Only 24 Scout Twins were sold and these were made specifically for mail order sales. The Super Wasp Twin, with rear facing plugs, was produced in two forms. The early models had rectangular exhaust ports, and the later ones had oval ports. Some 78 Super Wasps were produced altogether, together with a few flat fours. The Super Wasp had a new one-piece crankcase allowing for directly opposed cylinders, the con-rods being offset on the gudgeon pins. $\frac{3}{4}$ bhp at 10,000 rpm was achieved.

Bob Chunn in Nashville manufactured an early in-line SP alternate firing twin in 1938. The Chunn used many parts from the earlier Chunn Chum; bore and stroke were $\frac{5}{8}$ inch × $\frac{17}{32}$ inch and capacity ·32 cubic inch making a very small engine. The crankshaft was made out of sections which screwed into each other and were fixed with dowel pins. Con-rods had separate bearing straps. It was priced at $20. It would turn a 14-inch × 8-inch propeller at 5,000 rpm. Weight is 12 oz. It is estimated that perhaps fifty were produced altogether.

The Viking 65 was originally made by the Macval Mfg Co. of Burbank, California. Fig. 153 shows one of these engines, with a serial No. 1504. The crankcase is finished in red, and the motor is also fitted with a red anodised spinner nut and points cover. This engine, like all those twins discussed earlier in this chapter is arranged for simultaneous firing. An interesting design feature of the Viking 65 is that it features two small holes in both the front and rear of the off-side cylinder, which provide sub-piston induction for this cylinder only, and so help lean the fuel mixture to this cylinder, and thus help to equalise cylinder filling.

The Craftsman 9·95 cc twin (Fig. 154) was an Edgar T. Westbury design. They were manufactured by C. W. Juby and D. Braid of Craftsmanship Models Ltd, in Ipswich; but later, casting kits were also sold. All original factory-built motors are serial numbered, and are engraved with CML on the tops of the crankcases. The motor shown is No. 80901. The contact-breaker is driven from the rear of the crankshaft. Bore is ·750 inch and stroke ·688 inch. Compression ratio is 7:1 and weight 15 oz. The split crankcase is made from LAC 10 with phosphor bronze bearings. Power was ·2 bhp at 6,700 rpm.

The Elf range of engines, originally introduced in 1932, comprised the Corn Cob single, flat twin, flat four, and flat six. A considerable number were made in America, but few reached England due to relatively high cost factors. They remained in production up to 1950, and although most were petrol motors, a few glow plug versions were produced. Fig. 155 shows the classic 1948 flat four petrol motor of ·396 cubic inch capacity. This was the last model flat four petrol motor and used reed valve induction. Power was well below corresponding engines of similar capacity.

GHG produced a fine in-line alternate firing twin of 10 cc capacity before World War 2 (Fig. 65), but it only reached the prototype stage.

The 1944 Pal ·55 cubic inch, designed by P. Labeda was an interesting, well built alternate firing in-line petrol twin from Cedar Rapids, Iowa (Fig. 156). It was priced $62·50 when new. Bore was $\frac{3}{4}$ inch, stroke $\frac{5}{8}$ inch and weight 15 oz. The connecting rod was of tubular construction, made from a special alloy with light weight, but the tensile strength of steel. Rotary valve induction was incorporated, and more cylinder fins were machined on the upper parts of the cylinder than the lower parts, to equalise heat dissipation. A ball thrust bearing was incorporated. The contact breaker assembly was driven from the rear of the crankshaft, and the crankcase was of monoblock construction.

The Morton M-5 is probably the most famous multi-cylinder of all, but has been described previously under the four-stroke heading.

The Ace ·64 cubic inch twin, produced by John Kramer, who had been a machinist with Solar Aircraft Company, was conceived in 1944, and the first prototype, with rear facing plugs, manufactured in 1945. This original prototype had an induction system based on the 1928 Evinrude. The first production model Ace had a single carburettor and plugs fitted orthodoxly in the heads. Piston rings were fitted. The Ace ran at 9,500 rpm on a 12-inch × 6-inch propeller. These engines were manufactured by the Kramer-Grow Machine Co. of Satiago, California.

One of the earliest flat twin petrol engines marketed in 1932 was the 26 cc Camm, which was produced in England. Casting kits were marketed by Delaforce of London. The crankcase was split at the centre line and each half of this cast-iron unit was blind-bored. Both cylinders are diametrically opposed, and crank con-rods were incorporated. The motor utilised a flywheel type magneto mounted on the rear of the crank-shaft, while the prop driver was on the other end. The ignition system was unusual in that the spark plugs were connected in series, and in order to operate one plug was specially made as a double pole item.

Madewell, who are better known for their single cylinder engines, produced a few off-set flat twin side port engines, but these were really only in the prototype stage.

Another flat twin, produced in 1945 was the exceedingly interesting Howie twin, manufactured by Mr Howie of the HH Model Motor Co., of Norristown, Pennsylvania. H & H stood for Howie and Heuer. This motor, with a capacity of ·38 cubic inch was of the alternate filing configuration, but at the same time was a diametrically opposed flat twin! The formidable design problem with such a motor, of sealing each cylinder from the crankcase was solved by incorporating a Scotch Yoke. The connecting rods were rigidly mounted into the pistons, and were of circular section. They passed through a cylinder sealing plate in the lower liner and thence joined a banjo-shaped centre section, and at right angles to this section a slot was milled to contain a sliding block. This sliding block in turn was drilled to take the end of the crank pin. It can be seen, therefore, that when the engine fires only a force down the axis of the rigidly fixed con-rods is imparted to the yoke. This lateral motion is then converted into the rotary motion of the crankshaft by the sliding block. Workmanship is of a very high order. It will be noted that due to the cylinder sealing plates, no fuel mixture enters the crankcase centre section, and the yoke assembly is thus lubricated, with light oil, which fills the lower section of the crankcase, via a filler cap. Fuel mixture enters the cylinders via pipes, at the rear of each cylinder, from a common needle valve. The entire engine is very neat in appearance, and has a bore and stroke of ·625 inch.

The M & M Hurleman twin, produced by Herb Whal in Pennsylvania is an interesting petrol ignition flat twin, made up by using ·48 cubic inch Hurleman piston and liner units to give a total displacement of ·96 cubic inch. This limited production engine was introduced in 1973. With a 16-inch × 6-inch propeller and SAE 70 oil in a 1:3 fuel mixture, 5,200 rpm is available with the ignition in the neutral position. Price is $280, with engines being produced to order.

The 40 cc Condor Flat Four was one of the largest commercial model aero engines ever made. Produced before World War 2, it had a bore of 1 inch and stroke of ¾ inch. 1·6 bhp was claimed at 7,500 rpm. The engine had a cast iron crankcase, and the crankshaft ran on ball races. The opposed cylinders fired alternatively in pairs; and the distributor was mounted at the rear of the crankshaft.

(2) Diesel

The English Dragonfly Twin was one of the first twin cylinder diesel engines offered to the public, although Mills Bros had built an experimental V-Twin a few years earlier. The Dragonfly was an in-line alternate firing diesel, which was also sold, in component form, as a set of castings. The real exponent of the twin cylinder diesel was Herman Fricke of Cologne, who produced the excellent ball race simultaneous firing flat twins. These were known as the FMO Boxer engines, Boxer being the German term for a flat, simultaneous firing twin, where the pistons approach each other, and then fly apart again. Fig. 157 shows the 1959 FMO (Little Boxer) 3·5 cc. The shaft was carried on two ball races, and the carburettor was mounted on top. This engine was also fitted with a simple but effective multi-speed R/C carburettor as an optional extra. The engine ran very well, and extremely smoothly. The same basic design was scaled up, and marketed by Performance Kits in 5 and 6 cc versions in 1960. Both the 5 and 6 cc engines were available with an R/C throttle as an extra. The 6 cc developed ·7 bhp at 11,500 rpm and sold for £17 in 1961. A few FMO 9·2 cc diesels were also made, and these developed 1·2 bhp at 9,500 rpm using a 13-inch × 5½-inch propeller.

The PK Panther (Fig. 158) geared V-Twin was made in very small numbers, by the Moore Engineering Company of Leicester. This side port V-Twin used silver steel gears and a twin ball race crankshaft bearing on the main prop drive crankshaft. The motor was of side port configuration, and featured twin carburettors. It was a complex and expensive motor to make, but performed well in experienced hands. Capacity was only 1·5 cc, but the engine had very high torque characteristics, and would turn a 10-inch × 4-inch propeller. The motor was in production, as a prestige project in 1972, but only a few were made. This engine was developed from the earlier EmBee (Moore and Bailey) 1·5 cc flat geared twin (Fig. 136). The photograph shows the Mk 1 version of this engine, which was first marketed in 1969 and was in limited production for a few years, although due to continuous development it was rare to see two engines the same. These engines made a most interesting 'whirring' sound from the gears when running.

The Typhoon 7 cc (Fig. 159) from Veenhoven in Holland, had a ball race shaft and was of the alternate firing in-line type. The motor was imported into England by Performance Kits in 1960, but most of the motors were re-exported to America! In fact, only a few were sold, due to high price coupled with import duties.

The German Rupert Boxer flat twin was used in early competition R/C models and had an integral crankshaft driven pump, which was used to operate airdraulic servos. Fig. 160 shows one of these interesting engines. The design was taken over by the Webra company, who produced a similar motor with highly coloured anodised parts.

Col. Taplin produced the Taplin Twin alternate firing in-line diesels for some years in Kent, at the Birchington Engineering Company. Originally they used ED 3·46 pistons and liners, but subsequently the entire engine was made in their own works. Several versions of this engine were made, but most were of 7 cc capacity. The latter models had increased capacities, due to the demand for a greater power output. The engines were heavy but reliable and were mainly used in large R/C scale and C/L scale models. There was a marine conversion, which was very popular with boating enthusiasts, where the high weight penalty of this engine was of minor importance.

(3) Glow

The 1958 D-C Tornado 5 cc was produced in fair numbers for a twin. It could be fitted with exhaust stacks, as an extra, as in Fig. 161. Induction was via twin rotary shaft valves. The motor was used in the 580 square inch Performance Kits Pinnacle stunt control line model, and flew well except for the irritating habit of cutting out on its outer cylinder. The engines were packed, when new, in a distinctive triangular box, as were other D-C engines of the same period. The Tornado was nicely finished, with a vapour blasted crankcase, machined and polished cylinders and cylinder heads, and fully machined prop-driver and radial mount.

Northfield-Ross, designed by Lew Ross, produced some interesting glow twins. The 1974 ·60 in-line R/C alternate firing unit is shown in Fig. 162 but they also produced a flat ·61 twin, flat 4 and flat 6, all expressly for R/C use. See Figs 163, 164 and 165. The interesting in-line twin is only $4\frac{1}{2}$ inches long. Power is equivalent to a similar size orthodox single cylinder engine, but without the usual vibration. All-up weight is 16 oz. Bore is ·8 inch and stroke ·6 inch. Using a 14-inch × 6-inch propeller the revolution range is 2,200–9,000 rpm. The engine is supplied with a smart black anodised finish. The Flat 4 1·2 cubic inch develops 2·5 bhp at 15,000 rpm and the Flat 6 1·8 cubic inch gives 4 bhp at 15,000 rpm. These are probably the most powerful engines available to the modeller, at the time of writing. The con-rods of all these flat configuration engines are of the Desaxe type, being off-set on the gudgeon pins. In this way the opposing cylinders can be set diametrically opposite each other, giving a very compact arrangement.

The Wizard ·65 (Fig. 166) was produced as a conversion of the earlier Viking petrol engine, and the similarity can be seen by referring to the picture of the Viking shown in Fig. 153. The crankcase of the Wizard is fully polished, and the ignition parts removed. Serial number of the ·65 example shown is 1300.

Another excellent flat twin is the Shershaw Bantam ·60, specially designed for R/C use and produced in 1968. In 1971 an improved version of this same engine was marketed as the Bronner ·599, featuring coupled twin carbs.

In 1975, some of the finest multi-cylinder engines ever made were in production, manufactured by the old established Micron company in Paris. The Micron 2-24 of 4·9 cc gives ·4 bhp at 15,000 rpm. The recommended propeller is 10-inch × 6-inch. The exhaust stacks can be re-positioned by use of the special spanner provided. The crankshaft has two ball-bearings. All faces are surface machined, so obviating the use of gaskets (Fig. 167).

The last word is provided with the 1975 Micron 4-24 R/C model (Fig. 168), which was first introduced and imported into England by Performance Kits in 1973. This is a superb flat four. The front pair of cylinders fire simultaneously, followed by the simultaneous firing of the rear cylinders. Again all faces are surface machined and the twin ball race crankshaft is fitted. Capacity is 9·92 cc, bore 16 mm and stroke 12 mm.

Weight is 9·30 gm, and power output is ·8 bhp at 15,000 rpm. An 11-inch × 4-inch propeller is recommended. The 4-24 is provided with a pair of clack-valves, one for each pair of cylinders; it can thus be run in either direction. A Kavan R/C carburettor is fitted. This superlative engine is definitely a connoisseur's choice.

In Germany, a fine flat twin, also for R/C, and introduced in 1974, is the well-made Buco ·60. It can be considered as a continental equivalent of the Shershaw Bantam, and was produced for a similar market.

FMO produced the FMO Boxer Twins, developed from the earlier range of FMO diesels. They all followed the basic design of the 7·5 cc (Fig. 169) model illustrated. Other models were 8·2 cc, 10 cc and 16 cc versions. The 1970 10 cc model developed 1·2 bhp at 12,600 rpm. All were available with the special twin silencers illustrated and R/C throttle unit.

In 1975 Mr Norio Morita, in Japan, manufactured the Kamikaze in-line ·40 R/C twin. Bore is 16·6 mm and stroke 15 mm giving a capacity of 6·5 cc. The motor is illustrated in Fig. 170. A petrol ignition version is also made to order and this unit will turn a 13-inch × 5-inch propeller at 6,500 rpm. Price of the Glow version is $210. The Kamikaze, which means 'The wind of the gods', and is the mythical wind which protects Japan, was developed from the Strong 45 as made by Mr Shimizu in the mid 1960s. The Strong 45 was also an in-line twin; and was in fact developed from an even earlier in-line twin of 1940 vintage. The Kamikaze Glow model, in its latest form, will turn a Top-Flite 11-inch × 4-inch propeller at 10,000 rpm.

Over the years there have been many semi-commercial conversions of standard single cylinder engines into successful twins. The Cox-Haas flat simultaneous firing glow engine used Cox components, notably the Cox piston/cylinder units, the crankcase and crankshaft being built up to take them.

From Leicester, an EmBee glow geared twin was produced incorporating two geared Cox Golden Bee glow engines. These were arranged to drive a common ball-bearing mounted crankshaft. Price was very high and production very small.

Allyn produced two versions of their twin (2 inch × ·049 inch) Sky-Fury. This motor was of the in-line, alternate firing configuration. It could be mounted radially, or by a beam mount metal conversion. These engines were light, high revving, and were produced in quite large numbers (Fig. 171).

Pal Engineering of Cedar Rapids, Iowa, made an alternate firing glow twin of ·55 cubic inch known as the Pal 55G, with a bore of $\frac{3}{4}$ inch, stroke of $\frac{5}{8}$ inch and weight of 15 oz. It had a mono-block crankcase and rotary valve induction. Price was $49 for this model. The same engine, with throttle control carburettor was advertised at $64·50. This was known as the Pal 55CG. The ultra rare Pal 110 was a four cylinder version and was advertised at $115 complete with throttle. In this case, the cylinders were arranged to form a flat four. Bore and stroke was the same as the Pal 55. The engines could also be fitted with a reduction ratio prop drive. Care had to be taken with all Pal engines to cowl very carefully to avoid overheating the rear cylinders.

Pal Engineering marketed a special cowling, which was designed for this purpose.

The superb 1976 Micron M2-24 Bi-Cylindre, is of a similar layout to the PAL ·55, but is only of 4·96 cc. It is fitted with a R/C carb. Workmanship is of the very highest order, with surface machined joints throughout. Fig. 69 shows one of these engines fitted with a Rite-Pitch 10 × 6 laminated prop. The M2-24 retails at £239·88.

69

168

170

171

6 : CO_2 Engines

THESE engines used a CO_2 cartridge for power. With some designs such as the 1961 OK Cub, Weston and 1948 K the CO_2 cartridge was carried in the model, and the entire cartridge formed a fuel tank. Once released, the motor had to use up the entire Sparklet bulb. This proved expensive in fuel and, although the motors themselves were very light, the Sparklet bulb was heavy.

Following the early Campus engines, and the very similar Buzz, Mr Brown, of Brown Junior fame, devised a new Brown Junior CO_2 engine in 1970, which utilised its own fuel tank instead of the heavy sparklet bulb. This engine (Fig. 172) had its own lightweight tank, and is filled via the medium of a filler gun, which contains the sparklet capsule. The engine is incredibly light, and very powerful for its size. A flat twin CO_2 was also added to the Brown range in 1974. The single cylinder model has a capacity of ·005 cubic inch. By turning the cylinder head clockwise, revs can be increased, which at the same time increases the fuel consumption. The converse also applies. On test, one of these ·005 cubic inch Brown engines flew a 25-inch span PK Asteroid cabin model with ease, and, when mounted above the centre section on a power pod, it was just powerful enough to power a 29-inch span PK Owl sailplane.

In 1975 the Ticket Equipment Company of Cirencester, produced the Telco CO_2 engine, which was scheduled for large scale production. The engine was designed and developed by Mr Glenn Hargrave. This motor is the same capacity as the Brown, but utilises a plastic crankcase. This motor was extensively tested in a PK Owl which has a span of 29 inches. It would perform excellent ROG flights. Engine runs can be adjusted by means of an eccentric crankshaft bearing, which in turn alters the lift on the ball valve which meters the CO_2 flow. All-up weight, including tank, is only $\frac{1}{2}$ oz, and the engine run can be adjusted from 20–40 seconds, with the longer run giving less power for the longer period. To fill the tank, a specially developed Sparklet retaining gun is employed. The Sparklet is held in place, and its orifice opened with a spike; the gas is then retained by means of a non-return valve, which is depressed when it is pushed against the tank filler nipple (Fig. 204).

The production Telco CO_2 engine employing a plastic crankcase, rear cover plate and piston, is installed in the prototype PX 26-inch span Oclet F/F kit model illustrated in Fig. 196. The Telco, after extensive flight testing by Performance Kits, was distributed by them to the Model Trade to retail at £8·45 in 1976. The PK Oclet, demonstrated at the 1976 British Nationals, has had hundreds of excellent flights.

7: Pulse Jet Engines

THESE motors are very powerful and employ petal valves, together with trembler coil ignition. Due to the great thrust generated and the fact that they glow red hot in operation it is illegal to use them for free flight model aircraft: they are therefore restricted to speed control line flying. Originators of the system were probably the Dyna-Jet and Juggernaut Jet engines from America. A British-built motor, which was efficient but somewhat less powerful, was the Decca-Jet. The Tiger Jet from Italy was small and compact, and Rossi in Brescia, Italy, produced the very powerful Vulcan Jet. In 1962 the Vulcan had a static thrust of 3·5 kg. Length was 670 mm and all-up weight was 450 gm. Price in Britain was £17.

Typical specimens are illustrated in Fig. 173, which shows the petal valve Dyna-Jet, built from 1947 to the present day in Ohio, USA, and also the very similar OS Jet. To start these engines it was necessary to force air through the jet, using a high output stirrup pump.

The Sona Jet, which is a valveless tuned pipe, was made in Pennsylvania. Air was pumped through the front using a syringe, and starting effected by holding a flame near the exhaust. It ran on petrol.

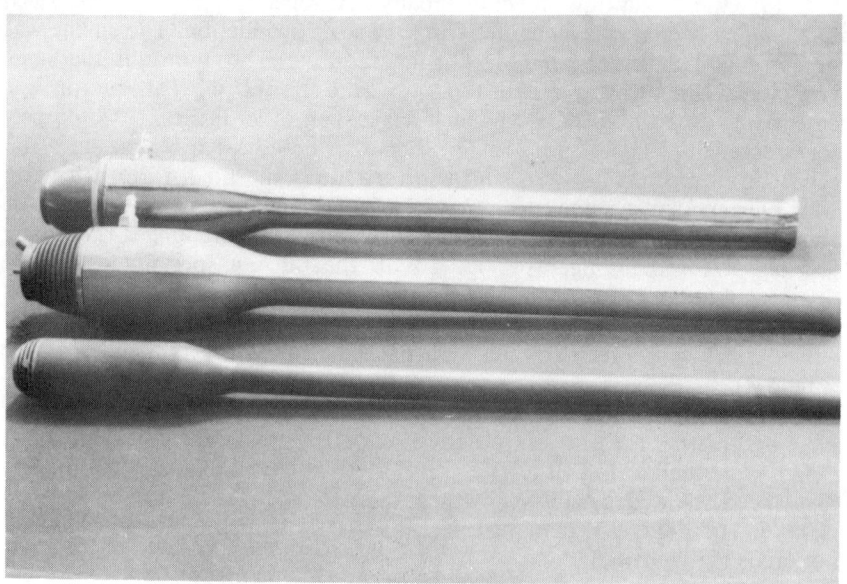

173

8 : Horizontal Piston Engines

THESE engines had the piston running parallel to the crankshaft. The most famous engine of this type (Fig. 174) is the 1964 Areo ·35 horizontal piston engine of ·35 cubic inch, which was originally designed for stunt C/L and was both powerful and exceedingly smooth in operation. Its low overall height encouraged neat cowling. An R/C model was produced later. The makers were the Aero Research & Development Co. of Buffalo, New York. The price of the motors, distributed by Performance Kits in Britain, was £15 15s 0d (£15·75).

Other engines using this configuration, although by differing actuation methods, were the 1941 Savage 60 petrol motor. Mr Savage was thought to have been the originator of the idea. The Savage, designed by Neil Savage was in limited production, and Mr Savage subsequently designed the Aero ·35. The Savage had the drive plate and cylinder head at opposite ends of the engine and this engendered problems of cooling and accessability to the spark plug.

In 1950 Clarence Lee designed the Lee In-Line Single. Only four were built using a Veco ·32 crankcase. K & B ·32 pistons and timers were incorporated. Weight was 5½ oz and power 11,000 rpm on a 10-inch × 6-inch propeller. The shaft drive plate and head faced the same way and the drive direction change was effected by gearing.

The Mac Engine, from Hertfordshire, used a system where the piston was in a straight line with the crankshaft, and was in fact co-axial with it. It was a most compact and ingenious layout. The Mac is a small glow engine of 1½ cc capacity, and looks like a small tube with a cylinder head on one end and prop driver on the other.

174

9: Mock Engines

THE EmBee ·75 mock rotary (Fig. 175) was derived from the EmBee ·75 Mk 3, but the side port induction tube was located in the starboard side of the crankcase, instead of at the rear. The exhaust port faced fore and aft and a dummy three-cylinder engine was fabricated and fixed behind the prop driver. In operation the inertia effect of the rotating mock three-cylinders closely resembled the full size type of rotary engine, particularly under a realistic cowling. Price was high and very few were made.

The 1949 Lionheart (Fig. 176) mock flat twin was marketed by Premier Model Aero Co. in Camden Town. Only one cylinder, of 2·48 cc was operative; the opposing one being a dummy, and acting as a fuel tank. It was intended for use in scale models, and was in very limited production.

175

176

10 : Jetex Rocket Engines

THE Jetex was originally produced by Wilmot, Mansour & Co. Ltd, of Totton, Hants, and was in considerable vogue when first produced. The first model produced was the Jetex 200 (Fig. 177), and the author used one of these to power a free flight model in 1951. Subsequent motors were the Jetex 100, 150, Scorpion, and 50.

All Jetex engines employed the same basic principal. Fuel in the form of solid, slow burning (and evil smelling) pellets from ICI was placed inside the body of the unit. A wick was coiled over the top surface of the pellet and passed through the edge of a wire mesh and thence through the jet orifice hole. The unit was then clipped together and the wick ignited with a match. When the fuel pellet ignited it burnt slowly, and the expanding gas, under pressure, was ejected through the jet, so producing the propulsion.

With the Jetex 200 illustrated, one or two pellets could be used to give a long or short engine run. It was important to score the second pellet to ensure ignition. Thrust was $1\frac{3}{4}$–2 oz. Maximum duration, 20–40 seconds. The five coil springs at the rear of the unit doubled as front plate retainers and a safety valve. The idea was that should the jet become blocked, the face plate would be allowed to lift against the spring pressure, thus allowing the gas to escape, and remove the danger of explosions. In practice the jet was never known to block in use, and the later models in the Jetex range ceased to use the complex multi-spring retaining arrangement.

The Jetex 50, produced in 1949, was the smallest motor in the Jetex range. It had a ribbed alloy motor casing, and was held together by a single clip. This motor was intended for use with small scale jet models.

177

11 : Electric Motors

THE basic problem with all past and current electric model aero power plants, as with those developed for motor cars, is that of a poor power/weight ratio of the overall power package.

Today's electric motors are very powerful when fitted with suitable reduction gearing; however, in spite of recent developments with Ni-Cad and Mallory type power cells, the battery weight required for adequate power is still on the high side.

The Mattel Superstar unit has recently been marketed with success. This unit utilises a small geared electric motor and has re-chargeable power cells. These in turn can be re-charged from a dry Lantern battery for 'on the flying field' charging.

For larger R/C-type models, commercial electric motors include the American Astro Flight unit. This has a specially wound armature and operates with direct drive as opposed to the more usual geared layout.

An example of the commercially produced geared system is the Alpha. This weighs 6·5 oz, and can be re-charged in 8 minutes. The engine run on one charge is 8 minutes. The motor is designed to operate on a 10-inch propeller. NICAD type batteries are utilised. Price quoted is $54·95. This unit is manufactured by Galler Electronic Industries, and has adequate power for radio controlled models.

In the summer of 1975 the Japanese Mabuchi Company produced the Aeromotor A1 unit. Weight was relatively low at $2\frac{1}{2}$ oz, and the motor, complete with batteries and charger was initially marketed at £7·25.

12 : Glow Plug Engines

(1) General

Ray Arden is usually given credit for inventing the glo-plug. The story is that while testing one of his high performance radially ported petrol engines he disconnected the ignition system, and found the engine kept running due to self detonation on a very hot spark plug.

The first glo-plugs were in fact modified spark plugs with a coiled platinum element instead of the usual spark electrodes. They were introduced in the autumn of 1948.

Arden ·19 glo-engines, fitted in such F/F competition pylon models as the Banshee were often winners.

Perhaps the honour as the first glo-engine should go to the H & H ·45. It was introduced in February 1947 at $24·50. The motor was of side port configuration, with what was described as hot coil ignition. The hot coil being incorporated at the rear of the cylinder head, was a built in feature. A 1½ volt starter battery was required. The engine went out of production with the introduction of the Arden.

At about the same time, but made in much smaller numbers, the Hetherington Meteor ·23 glo-engine was introduced by the old established Hetherington Company of Eagle Rock Boulevard, in Los Angeles, who had sold model aero engines since 1933. This unusual engine used FRV and the same unique fabricated metal constructional techniques as the earlier Hetherington ·23 petrol engine (see Fig. 38). One of the last ·23 glo-engines is illustrated in Fig. 178.

A great number of early glo-engines were simply ignition engines with a glo-plug substituted for the spark plug, and with the contact points omitted. Such engines were produced by Ohlsson and Rice, who crimped a metal cover over the front shaft where the points would have been previously fitted. The OK Herkimer Co. of New York also carried out large numbers of similar factory conversions.

Some motors due to their robust construction were very suitable for conversion; such an engine was the Buch Contestor SP 10 cc. All that was required was to fit a ⅜-inch glo-plug and fly!

In England most glo-plug engines were designed from scratch. International Model Aircraft produced the Frog 160 of 1·6 cc (Fig. 179) and Allbon, in 1949, made the 1·49 cc Arrow. DC, however, produced a conversion head for their first engine, the 5 cc DC Wildcat, and a conversion head was also available for the DC 3·50 diesel, which was then known as the DC 350 G. (Fig. 106). The Frog 500 G, however, was in fact marketed before the Frog 500 P petrol engine, and is perhaps the only case where the Glo variant was produced before the petrol model. Very few petrol versions were made. This engine bore a strong resemblance to the K & B Torpedo ·29 of the same period. Fig. 180 shows the Frog 500 G.

The Exeter 10 cc (Fig. 181) was a small production glo-engine, featuring a very small diameter ball race crankshaft. It bears a strong resemblance to the Arden in general layout. Very few of these engines were in fact produced.

The K Engineering Co. of Gravesend in Kent produced an inexpensive glo FRV 1·9 cc unit called the K Tornado; this was an adaption of their popular Kestrel engine (Fig. 83).

The OK Herkimer Co. produced a large range of OK glo-engines designated OK Cub. A typical specimen is the OK Cub ·19 cubic inch, illustrated in Fig. 182. OK design features, often incorporated with their engines, are compact overall size with finely machined fins in unit with the cylinder liner and the distinctive screw on hexagonal head. OK produced glo-engines from ·049–·35 cubic inches.

The Larson Royal 05, produced in Seattle in 1948, was probably the first $\frac{1}{2}$ A glo-engine. It was a very well made motor featuring a long crankshaft and front rotary shaft induction. It was intended primarily for use with scale models, and hence the long shaft. The Royal 05, made in small numbers, sold mainly in the Seattle area for about $10. The introduction of the mass produced K & B Infant destroyed the market for the Royal.

Following the earlier DC Wildcat glo-model, which was in fact a DC Mk 3 with glo-head, and the Allbon Arrow 1·49, mentioned earlier, Davies-Charlton introduced the Bantam ·049 in 1959. It was also sold in de-luxe form with a radial mount tank from 1962 onwards. This was the cheapest and largest selling glo-motor in England, until it was replaced in 1971 by the DC Wasp ·049, which has a much better performance. This engine is also available with the radial mount tank. Price was £3·17 in 1975, and the motor is a top seller. Fig. 183 shows the engine in a specially designed Performance Kits Wasp Wings kit. Power is such that a lightweight R/C can readily be fitted in this model by an experienced builder. The Wasp was also marketed up to 1974 as the Frog 049 Venom. In this guise it had the radial tank fitted and both this and the cylinder head were anodised red.

Bill Atwood who was a prolific engine designer was responsible for the Atwood ·049 Cadet (Fig. 184) and also the popular and better known Atwood Wasp; both engines were very light and powerful. As will be seen, the Cadet used the rear crankcase cover retaining bolts to double as radial mounting bolts. A $\frac{1}{4}$-inch detachable glow plug is fitted.

One of the last engines produced by O & R was the O & R Midjet ·049 (Fig. 185). This was a well made little engine; but was more complex to build, and possessed less power than some of its competitors. A bad design feature was the way the needle valve was arranged so that it must pass through the engine bearers.

Dynamic Models Inc., who made the Johnson engines produced the truly excellent little Holland Hornet glow $\frac{1}{2}$A motors, with the plug forming an integral part of the cylinder head. This provided a hemispherical combustion chamber. ·049, ·051, and ·051 R/C motors were produced.

The Gilbert ·07 and ·11 engines (Fig. 186) also feature the integral glow head. These were side port engines and featured starter re-coil springs located inside cast prop driver plate housings. These engines were designed for use with ready-to-fly plastic C/L models, but were also available as separate entities, and were intended for the beginners low price market. The original production motors had considerable trouble with piston/bore fits; but those made afterward, without the starter, ran quite well.

Fig. 187, shows the rare Danish Viking 2·5 G rear rotary disc motor. It uses twin transfers and twin exhausts set at right angles to each other.

The 1959 Pagco Pagliuso XF-9 ·09 cubic inch (Fig. 188) was originally designed for a ready-to-fly plastic C/L model of a VTO type aircraft, complete with exhaust restrictor type throttle. It is a highly finished little motor with a long crankshaft and extended choke tube facing downwards below the shaft. These features combine to make it particularly suitable for scale models.

(2) Stunt Glow Engines of ·30–·59 cubic inches

Many glow engines were designed especially for stunt C/L work. Such a motor was the original sandcast Fox 35. The Johnson ·35, ·32 and ·29 engines and the lovely 1961 Johnson Stunt Supreme ·36 were developed from the earlier Orwick and Cunningham petrol engines. As a point of interest the Orwick engines could always be recognised from the Cunninghams by the fact that their crankcases were enamelled apple green, while the Cunninghams were blue. The Johnson Stunt Supreme had an exceptionally large crankshaft diameter, and this in turn allowed it to incorporate an exceptionally large shaft rotary intake port, and was one of the factors which determined the above average power output from this motor. One of these engines was used to fly the Performance Kits Pinnacle Mk E-54, featured in Fig. 189. This model had a wing area of 580 square inches, and had considerable competition success.

Perhaps the first really good English glow engine was the original Yulon ·30 (Fig. 190). The makers were Messrs Yule & Long. This engine with its distinctive appearance, light weight and good power/weight ratio, was the natural choice for stunt C/L flyers, and was the engine chosen for one of the Gold Trophy winners. It had curious multi-hole exhaust ports, and 360° porting. The Yulon ·30 was probably the best, from a quality standpoint, of the Yulon range, which was later expanded to include the Yulon ·29 (Fig. 191), Yulon ·49 and finally the Yulon Eagle (Fig. 192). All used the same crankcase casting, with black crackle paint finish; but the head fins were machined in such a way as to give the finished product a completely different appearance. The crackle finish was also omitted from the Eagle. The Yulon ·49 was simply a scaled up version of the Beehive ·29 motor. The ·30, ·29, and ·49 all had hexagonal prop drivers machined from bar stock. The Eagle finally abandoned the multi-hole exhaust porting and used the more traditional 360° exhaust, with four large ports, and considerable sub-piston induction. The Eagle also had a traditional prop drive plate, and simple prop nut, instead of the more elegant items featured on the earlier models. The Eagle was the last motor produced by the Yulon Company before production ceased. Just before they stopped trading, a 2·5 cc prototype was constructed, which although it had the same power as the then current Oliver, lacked the latter's ease of handling and lower speed torque characteristics.

The green head K & B ·201, originally designed for combat C/L in America, was used by the author to fly the negative stagger Lynx Mk 14 (Fig. 193), in 1963.

From Australia Gordon Burford & Co. originally produced the Sabre range of ·29 and ·35 Glow engines; but the name was soon changed to Glow Chief. Over the years ·29, ·35, and ·49 glow engines were made. Fig. 194 shows a Glo-Chief ·35 Mk 2 plain bearing stunt motor in an Eclipse Mk 48 of 1958 vintage, which was a winner at many stunt C/L competitions in its day. Early Sabre and Glo-Chief engines had plain cast cylinder head fins, but the Mk 2 series used fully machined head fins, which were anodised metallic orange. The last Glo-Chief ·35 stunt engine was the excellent twin BR unit shown in Fig. 195 and flown in the Gold Trophy at the British Nationals in 1963, when it powered a 40-inch span Lynx 15 negative stagger bi-plane with 593 square inches of wing area. This motor was fitted with a Grish 9-inch × 6-inch three blade propeller to reduce the undercarriage length, and consequential inertia forces, to a minimum.

The 1960 Micron ·29 stunt engine, giving ·55 bhp at 15,000 rpm was known as the Super Sport (Fig. 22) and was also used in the Gold Trophy and other C/L events. It is an excellently engineered 5 cc engine, with a sandcast crankcase, and surface jet needle valve assembly. The surface jet system is widely used in 1975 on the well made mass produced Cox engines, which are machined from solid extrusions. L. M. Cox originally marketed these engines under the name of Thimble Drome, when they were intended for use with model racing cars.

GHG produced a few 4 cc glo engines for stunt C/L work and one of these is shown in Fig. 68; it used the multi-hole exhaust port system, as featured in the Yulon 30.

One of the latest stunt C/L engines to be produced is the truly excellent 1974 Micron Meteor 51A with ·9 bhp available and a capacity of 8·31 cc. It is also available in R/C form. The special stunt motor is shown in Fig. 197. Other Micron Stunt engines include the M29, M35, and M45. These are plain bearing front rotary units. The numbers denote the capacities in cubic inches. Thus the M35 is ·35 cubic inch. Power outputs range from ·5–·6 bhp. Quality, as with all Micron engines, is excellent, and price is accordingly very high.

(3) Speed and Team Racing Engines

Early speed models were nearly always control liners, although the author built some speed F/F models such as the 1948–49 Meson Mk 1 and Mk 2, powered with an ED Racer 2·46 Mk 1 unit. McCoy ·60, 1947/9, Ball ·604, 1948/49 Bungay 600, ZN ·60, Hornet ·60, and 1948 Rowell ·60 from Dundee, were all specifically designed for C/L speed work, although the Rowell could also be purchased with an extended crankshaft and spur gearing for use with model racing cars. All the above were typical speed type engines, as was the Nordec RG 60 (Fig. 198), of 10 cc. The Nordec, produced by the North Downs Engineering Co. was developed from the earlier petrol version and bore a close resemblance to the McCoy. The Nordec RG 60 features rear rotary disc induction and a twin ball race crankshaft. Workmanship was of a high order throughout and the whole engine was held together with Allen screws. The crankcase was nicely finished in black crackle and the head highly polished. Nordec is formed in relief on the transfer port, and the motor shown is serial No. 427. The high deflection piston used twin piston rings. A specially prepared Nordec achieved the speed of 116 mph. It may be of interest to note that the North Downs Engineering Co. were also manufacturers of the well-known Nordec superchargers, which were fitted to sports cars of the same period.

The Dooling ·29, and ·61 (Fig. 199) engines, produced by Dooling Bros in California, were specially designed for speed C/L work. The ·29 claimed ·75 bhp at 17,500 rpm, although as the more powerful Carter 5 only produced ·595 bhp at 18,000 rpm on test, maybe the Dooling claim was somewhat optimistic. Both engines were finely finished, the Dooling ·29 having an excellent vapour blasted pressure die-cast crankcase. The author used one of these Dooling ·29 engines for both a 6-ft span competition F/F flying wing, called the Ionosphere Mk 6 in 1951, which had many flights on Fairlop Aerodrome; and also in 1952 to power the Flying Mist 3-ft span all-wing type C/L model. Difficulty was experienced due to the large transfer and crankcase volumes, which led to low volumetric efficiency and consequential low fuel draw characteristics. Fitted with the correct pressurised fuel feed, they performed admirably, and were in fact very good motors.

The Dooling ·61, which for some years was the top C/L engine was produced in A and B series; both had the same capacity of ·607 cubic inch; but the earlier A series can be identified by the fact that it had more fins on the cylinder. Fig. 199 shows a superb example of the B series motor, which was manufactured in 1947. The crankshaft was produced in three pieces, composed of the main shaft, the crank-web, and the crank pin. The web is located with a dowel pin. The forged alloy con-rod featured a steel insert for its needle roller big-end bearing (serial No. 1785).

In the early 1950s, 192 mph was unofficially claimed for a speed C/L model using one of these engines running with oxygen injection. 160 mph was readily available using traditional speed fuel. All Dooling engines were produced between 1947–63.

A yellow anodised, vertically ribbed, exchange crankcase was made as a replacement for the original Dooling ·61 crankcase, and was known as the 'yellow jacket' Dooling. This crankcase was manufactured by an outside supplier.

The Carter 5, produced for English speed competition C/L models, by Mr Fred Carter, was a carefully reworked Dooling ·29 with largely new internal components. An interesting feature was that the Carter 5 had smaller exhaust ports in the liner but larger transfer ports. The fuel used was equal parts of Methanol and Nitro Methane with 20% Castrol 'R' Castor based oil. Power was ·595 bhp at 18,000 rpm.

Fig. 200 shows the well made and powerful Rossi ·60, made in Italy in 1963. It was also sold in a specially tuned and chromed form. An R/C version of the same motor was in production at the same time. Power output was 1·84 bhp at 18,500 rpm.

The characteristics of the C/L team racing engine was different from the all out speed unit in that fuel consumption became a matter for concern. The Dooling ·29 was not ideal for T/R use due to its very high consumption. The Eta ·29, made by Eta Instruments in Watford, Herts, was developed for class B T/R work as was the Johnson ·29 and many others.

In the search for still greater power the Komet ·15 (Fig. 201) speed engine was designed to use a tuned exhaust pipe muffler, and this system is used by most modern speed engines, such as the Italian OPS.

In about 1947, ERE (English Racing Engine) produced a diesel, marketed by Replica of Sloane Street, London, to compete in Class Speed Competitions. It was very well made, but was not competitive, and very few were manufactured. The ERE was one of the first diesels to feature a standardised locking lever to lock the compression vernier in place, and to stop it from loosing its setting when the motor was running, lightly loaded with speed propellers.

A rare Dutch engine, made in small numbers was the Favoriet 2·47 cc, which was manufactured by Thuella Miniature Motors. It was oversquare with a stroke of 14·45 mm, and a bore of 14·75 mm; all-up weight was 145 gm. Maximum power output was ·26 bhp at 13,000 rpm and maximum torque was ·019 kg at 7,000 rpm. The motor had a combined beam and radial mounting system. The rear cover plate, which had the intake tube passing through it, was located to the back of the crankcase with four locating bolts. These were arranged in a square, so that the rear cover plate could be rotated through 90° thus providing a radial mount with the plate in the horizontal position, or beam mounting in the vertical position. When it was mounted vertically, traditional beam mounting lugs, cast in unit with the crankcase, were exposed.

Fig. 205, shows one of these engines, serial No. S67. With the rear cover plate removed, one can observe the fully machined con-rod and heavily counterbalanced, one-piece crankshaft. There is one ball race fitted just in front of the crank-throw. Mounted in unit with the cover plate is a plastic clack valve, which is spring loaded in the closed position. The valve is held in alignment by a retaining cage, bent up from sheet brass, the hollow top of which is pressed in to retain the valve spring. The red anodised cylinder head locates the cylinder liner in position with three long bolts, which are threaded into small lugs in the top of the crankcase. The inside of head bears on the top of the liner, and holds an annular projection on the liner, just below the exhaust ports, in position against an annular groove machined inside the crankcase. The motor is fitted with a nylon washer, behind the prop driver, and this limits crankshaft end play. In Holland this item is called a drukring. The Favoriet was in production in 1960–61 and only about 150 of them were made.

With team racing as opposed to speed C/L flying fuel consumption was of considerable importance. With early team race models this importance was exaggerated due to the fact that the pit crew, who were responsible for starting the engine, often experienced great difficulty with this task; and so in order to reduce the number of pit stops, and the related number of engine starts, low power and low consumption engines, such as the ED 3·46 were often used.

With experience, and greater expertise gained in handling their motors, the engine starting time was very considerably reduced, and more powerful motors came into vogue. Such engines as the Amco 3·5 PB were used at first, but when the rules were finalised, and team racing divided into two classes referred to as Class A and Class B, the maximum engine capacity was fixed at 2·5 cc and 5 cc respectively. The 2·5 cc class was dominated for some years by the Oliver Tiger, which combined relatively high output, with ease of handling and moderate thirst. The Rivers Silver Streak, in tuned form also won a number of Class A events. Early Class B events were dominated by the Eta ·29 glow engine. In more recent times the Czech state-owned MVVS company have had success with their 2·5 cc Schneürle port T/R diesel. Glow engines have dominated Class B events from early times due to the fact that the few large, powerful diesels, such as the ED Miles Special and the Typhoon 5 cc, were both heavy and physically bulky, thus increasing drag, due to over-size fuselage widths. Ultimate power was usually less than their equivalent glow counterparts.

(4) FAI 2·5 cc Engines

In recent years, in an effort to rationalise the many engine sizes for International Competitions, the Federation Aeronautique International which is the international body governing model aircraft competitions, has specified the 2·5 cc engine as the most suitable for competitive events, such as C/L combat, Free Flight, and Class A team racing, etc. For this reason a great deal of effort has been put into this size of engine.

John Oliver, the producer of the Oliver Tiger engines, has specialised in this class for many years, starting with the Raylite Panther 2·5 cc side port diesel, produced in Nottingham.

Gig Eifflaender of Progress Aero Works, who produces the PAW engines in Macclesfield, started with the plain bearing Eifflaender 2·5 cc diesel. Subsequently his engines were all called PAW motors, and bear a strong family resemblance to each other, to this day. PAW 1·49, 2·49, and 3·2 cc (1·19 cubic inch) engines are produced. These latter were intended for combat C/L flying, and the ·19 D motor was at one time marketed as the Combat Special. The earliest PAW 2·5 motors had a prop drive formed so that its sides folded back over the front shaft housing, so keeping dirt from entering the bearing during contact with the ground as a result of combat flying. In 1975 the PAW production range was made up of the 1·49-DS, 2·49-DS, and 19-DS engines. All these are available with exhaust mufflers, which can be obtained as extras. Fig. 122 shows a 1975 PAW 249-DS.

One of the most powerful early FAI class engines was the German Webra Mach 1 2·5 cc twin BR diesel, much used for all types of FAI competition events. The author used one of these engines to power the Performance Kits Proton Mk 10 in 1958. This was a swept forward wing, combat, all wing model, with a wing span of 26 inches.

Today the diesel is still favoured for combat and team racing, due to its good specific consumption figures, and easy starting; but free flight modellers tend to favour the glow racing engine for ultimate power output.

Gordon Burford, maker of Taipan, made very powerful 2·5 cc BR racing diesels up to 1974. Micron, in 1974–75 produced a competition 2.48 cc BR diesel, built to their usual high standard. Like all Micron's it is expensive but very good. Fig. 144 shows one of these engines. One side of the crankcase is inscribed with MM, which stands for Moteurs Micron, and the other side with 2·5 and a R to indicate its capacity, and that it is a 'Racing' motor.

(5) R/C Glow Engines

With the growing popularity of R/C, engines were specially designed for this purpose. Some of the first were the Glow-Chief ·19 R/C and the Japanese Kyowa ·45 R/C. These engines featured a rotating needle valve assembly, coupled to an exhaust swivel blanking plate. The rotating spray bar caused problems with the fuel tubing connection over the full throttle range.

With the development of proportional R/C these early variable speed carburettors proved inadequate. The next phase in R/C carburettor design is shown in Fig. 207, which depicts a Tono ·35 R/C ball race glow engine; this engine also features an unusual twin plug head. The plug threads also differ from the usual ¼-inch 32 tpi pattern. The fuel feed union remains fixed. There are screws to progressively control the fully open and closed choke positions, together with a supplementary air intake for idling purposes. The piece of wire and seal, securing the cylinder head fins to the crankcase, are to ensure that the engine is not dismantled when the engine is returned for work under guarantee. The engine illustrated is serial No. 2708, and Tono is inscribed in large lettering on the outside of the transfer port.

With the lessening interest in stunt C/L and the demise of the Glow-Chief engines, Gordon Burford decided to call all his engines Taipan. He produced a number of excellent ball race ·61 R/C engines, under this name, to compete with the more common OS., Enya, Merco, and Fuji products.

For Pylon-R/C racing a ·40 cubic inch motor with more power is required; and as with the earlier C/L speed engines, racing type units have been produced. Taipan currently produce an excellent Schneurle-ported ·15 cubic inch, and 3·5 cc unit, and in 1975 a ·40 cubic inch was in a prototype stage. Other competition R/C stunt (pattern) and Pylon racing engines are the Austrian HP and HB who produce ·61 and ·40 class engines for use with aerobatic and pylon racing planes respectively. There is also the Japanese OS ·40 and the American K & B ·40. Ross Power Inc. produced the very powerful ·61 R/C Custom engine in 1974. Using Schneurle porting, 1½ bhp is claimed. The liner is chrome plated. Weight 15 oz, bore/stroke ratio 1:1, price $115. At the bottom end of the price scale is the Japanese Ueda ·60, with curious squared off crankcase, and stylised rectangular transfer ports. Most of the Ueda range of motors features similar styling.

For aerobatic R/C flying, low speed torque is important, as is good volumetric efficiency. The excellent Micron 3·5 R/C and ·45 R/C engines are shown fitted into low speed aerobatic Sun Bird kits. These negative stagger semi-ducted wing design 51-inch span kits were marketed in January 1973. The Micron engines proved to be absolutely reliable (see Fig. 208/9). The ·45 engine is fitted with a Super-Tigre extractor type silencer, as opposed to the Standard Micron expansion type unit.

Engines of the Schneurle port type, with rear facing exhausts, which have been specially developed in 1974 for Pylon racing, are the Super Tigre X-40, selling at $65, which has won several important Pylon race competitions, and the OPS 40, both made in Italy.

The OPS ·40 claims 1·2 bhp at 20,000 rpm. Both are well made racing engines. Another excellent motor to use the Schneurle port layout is the Micron ·21 twin BR R/C engine. Again the exhaust is at the rear, but the motor is not in the competition market, being an unusual size. Capacity is 3·26 cc and the power ·35 bhp. Rev range is 2,500–14,000 rpm (see Fig. 210). The exclusive Micron type needle valve should be noted. This has been used on all Micron engines since they started production. The needle itself is threaded into the spray bar body, and is locked against the outside of the thimble slotted friction casing with a small nut. A coil spring, wound round the exterior of the thimble casing ensures that a good interference friction fit is made with the outside of the brass spray bar body. The system is extremely effective and pleasant to operate. A special transverse silencer is also made specially for this engine.

In the summer of 1975 two giant R/C glow units were put on the British market in the form of the Moki 25 cc and the Kolbe Rhino 25 cc; this latter comes complete with 20-inch × 5-inch propeller (Fig. 215). Both these motors are intended for use with very large scale models. The Rhino is on the left, and is fitted with a silencer; it also comes with its own radial mount.

(6) R/C Diesel Engines

Not many diesel engines are produced specifically for R/C because the large glow motor tends to be lighter, easier starting and smoother running. In 1974 Moore Engineering in the Isle of Man produced two good little R/C engines. These are the ME Heron 1 cc R/C and the ME 1·5 R/C Snipe. Both motors are of course intended for sports flying.

The Taplin Twin and FMO Boxer diesel R/C twins have been covered on pp 51 and 53 respectively, and were of course originally developed for R/C applications. The ED Miles Special 5 cc diesel could also be obtained with an R/C throttle unit, as an optional extra, and a similar R/C conversion unit was made available for the Jena 2·5 cc ball race engine, previously discussed.

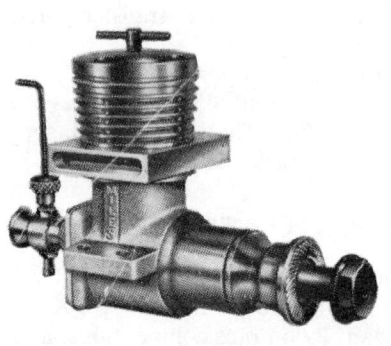

94

96

139

169

13 : Replica and Semi-collectors' Engines

IN recent years, due to the vastly increased interest in all types of model engines, together with the formation of the Model Engine Collectors Association, and the International Aero Engine Collectors Society, there has been a great increase in demand for some of the older and rarer model aero engines, both for collectors and for vintage flying enthusiasts. To fill this demand some of these engines have once again been put into limited production, sometimes using some of the left over original parts. Such engines as the Super Cyclone, and Anderson Spitfire have been re-produced by Remco in Colorado, who also manufactured in 1971 a Remco ·29, which is very reminiscent of a K & B ·29. The Remco has a bore of ·725 inch and stroke of ·724 inch. Fig. 211 shows the author's example, which bears the serial No. 285. The serial numbers on these Remco ·29 engines are the same as the MECA membership numbers of their owners. Remco also make the ¼-inch spark plug, as supplied with the motor. External finish is of a high order. The crankcase is vapour blasted, and the tank, cylinder-head, drive disc, and timer housing are anodised blue.

Fig. 7 shows a replica hex-head Brat ·14 cubic inch, made by Carl Carlsson in San Jose, California. It is fitted into a 50-inch span Performance Kits Model L Sports Model, and performs very well. This engine sold for $56·95 in de luxe form in 1973, and is an exact replica of the original Jack Keener design, produced in 1937. Bore is ·534 inch and stroke ·618 inch. It will do 7,000 rpm with an 8-inch × 5-inch propeller, but as illustrated it is fitted with a 9-inch × 5-inch. The actual engine and plane in Fig. 7 took part in the 1973 Society of Antique Modellers Championships in Taft, California. Only 100 of these engines were produced.

Due to the extensive hand work required to produce these replica engines, they are, of necessity very expensive, and usually cost at least as much as an original example of the same engine. They are collectors engines in their own right.

In recent years, the Doonside Mills ·75, promoted by Ivor Stowe, and manufactured by G. Burford of Taipan in Australia, has been marketed, due to the great demand for the ever popular Mills ·75. This engine is quite as good as the original, and is illustrated in Fig. 212. The Doonside version has Australia neatly inscribed on the rear cover plate, and differs from the original in having a cast, in front transfer port and four shaft housing stiffening webs. The engine illustrated which is serial No. 288, has a green anodised cylinder head, although they were anodised in various colours. The fuel tank is opaque by comparison with the original, and the needle valve housing has been squared off. A more pronounced venturi is featured, and the crankcase itself is bright alloy, as opposed to the black painted magnesium of the originals.

Nearly all Mills ·75 Replica type motors have been the very popular and well known Mills ·75 Mk 2; however in November 1975 the first three production prototypes of the Hobbs ·75 were running satisfactorily. The Hobbs ·75 manufactured by Tracel Ltd, of Great Gransden, is similar to the Mills ·75 Mk 1 motor. The crankcase is machined from an extrusion, and is of the Mk 1 1·3 rectangular type section. The entire motor is machined from alloy, and duly polished. On test, it was found that one of these motors, which was still rather tight, would turn a 7-inch × 4-inch propeller at 9,000 rpm. The same motor was subsequently fitted into a PK Ion kit, and test flown on Biggleswade Common. Fig. 220 shows two of the first three prototype motors produced.

In 1974–75 a few Mills ·75 engines were produced in India from the original dies and a number of these have been imported into Britain. Fig. 213 shows one of these ·75 Indian motors (serial No. AH 138). The crankcase is sandcast and grey in colour. The rear cover plate is machined from dural, as opposed to the cast magnesium component of the original, and it is tightened by means of two $\frac{1}{8}$-inch diameter holes, drilled to take an assembly key. The prop nut, though similar in design to the original, is of smaller diameter.

Performance of both the Doonside Mills and the Indian Mills are roughly equivalent to that of the original. The Doonside model has a slightly superior exterior finish. Later versions of the Indian model also leave something to be desired from a workmanship point of view and lack of quality control.

In California, the Apex 120 has recently been reintroduced. This is a modern replica of an engine which closely resembled the Foster ·99 cubic inch petrol motor of the same period, and is built to a very high standard by John Nuovo. The Foster was one of the largest mass produced aero model engines, and is of side port configuration. Many are still in use in American Old Timer events. The Apex 120, however, can be readily recognised by its sandcast crankcase. In 1975 M & G engines of Denver, Colorado, proposed to reintroduce the Foster ·99, using original crankcases. They also propose to make replicas of other Foster's should the demand prove sufficient.

Originally produced by F. Tlush in 1936 in Lyndhurst, New Jersey, the Tlush Super Ace has been re-introduced, in small quantities, for the benefit of collectors. The replica Tlush motors use many of the remaining parts, and are made under the supervision of the original designer. Both the original and the replica are built to a very high standard.

A number of engines have been produced around the World which are nearer to imitations than what could strictly be defined as Replica engines. These have beeen produced for the local market, sometimes simultaneously, in the absence of the original product. It is said that imitation is the sincerest form of flattery; and two engines are mentioned to illustrate this point. In both cases the original to be imitated is the excellent Dooling ·61 speed engine (Fig. 199), and its imitators, both excellent motors, are the Swiss Amro 10 cc and the Swedish Komet 10, made by Mr R. Johansson in Vasteras, who started building engines in 1944–6 with a 2·06 cc SP diesel called after the town, and showing a strong Dyno influence. A contemporary Dyno-influenced diesel of the same period, was the small production Swedish TFA.

In 1975, the MVVS company, in Czechoslovakia, produced, as a replica collectors item a batch of 30 6·2 cc BE-961 diesels, which originally date to 1941-6. This is a heavy motor, of the in-line alternate firing type of diesel. An interesting feature is that the contra-pistons are simultaneously adjusted via common spur gearing of their comp. screws.

216

217

215

Fig. 217 above is interesting in that the author cannot identify it. Perhaps some reader can do so?

14: Propellers

MANY early model aero engines were supplied with the maker's own propellers. These were specifically designed for use with the typical slow flying FF model for which the engines were intended. For example, the OK Twin had a Hydulignum 20-inch × 6-inch propeller. This also ensured that the revs did not rise to the point where the welded crankshaft would disintegrate!

The Mills 1·3 Mk I, of which more than 20,000 were made, had a Hydulignum propeller of $9\frac{1}{2}$ inches × 5 inches. The first figure represents the diameter from tip to tip and the latter the pitch. This is the distance the propeller would cut into soft butter if it revolved slowly through one revolution.

With the development and expansion of the hobby, and the greater specialisation in types of engines, so the propellers were designed for specific combinations of model aircraft and engines. Thus Speed Models used small diameter, higher pitch propellers, sometimes called 'tooth picks', to enable the engines to operate in the rpm range where they develop maximum power.

For C/L stunt flyers, the traditional propeller for a ·35 cubic inch powered 580 square inch model, such as the PK Pinnacle, would be a medium blade area 10-inch × 6-inch propeller.

In the early days of C/L flying, when many large diesels were in use, 'club-ended' propellers were developed, not for their aerodynamic efficiency, but to increase the inertia of the propeller, and to aid starting with these high compression diesels. Such a propeller was commercially produced by Pinnacle Propellers, which were made by the Southern Junior Aircraft Co., in Brighton.

Most early propellers were made from woods such as Beech, Maple, and Mahogany, although a few were made from Walnut. Sometimes they were laminated for elegance and strength and sometimes cut from Hydulignum, which was a compressed multi-wood layer laminate, of great strength.

Some early propellers, such as that used on the Comet ·18 petrol engine were carved from aluminium, and a stamped sheet duralumin 8 inch × 6 inch, called the Duraprop was marketed for use with the Mills 1·3. Up to about 7,000 rpm these propellers were reasonably safe; but above this rev range the aluminium tends to crystalise at the blade roots, and the blades part company with the propeller hub, with disastrous results.

Early plastic propellers, such as the Tru-Flex, which were popular in the late 1940s and early 1950s, suffered the same fate, as revs and engine performance improved.

A few variable pitch propellers have been made over the years, such as that sold with the Morton M-5 (Fig. 46); this is of aluminium and can be pre-set to the desired pitch before a flight. Great care must be taken to equalise pitch angles.

Nylon was next on the scene, and this material, particularly when annealled, raised the safe rev range still further. If the nylon has not already been annealled, this can be done by immersing the propeller in glycerine at 170°C for a period of 5 minutes. One of the first quality nylon propellers was the French HS, made with black Nylon-Rislan. Recent developments have been the insertion of glass fibre into the nylon before moulding. This has successfully been done with the Taipan prop range. Fig. 214 shows an assortment of propellers, covering a number of types marketed in the last thirty years. The total number of combinations and permutations is of course very great indeed.

Wooden airscrews have always been in production during this period. In 1960 the Australian Strato propellers produced a fine range of Celery Pine and Myrtle wood plastic coated airscrews. Today the old Stant and True-pitch propellers have gone, but the modeller has a vast range of excellent propellers to choose from, made by manufacturers such as Grish, Punctillio, Top Flight, X-Pert and Y & O Rite-Pitch to name a few.

Propeller Engine Chart

The following engine capacity/propeller size table has been designed to give a rough guide as to the correct propeller size for a given engine capacity. It will be appreciated that the propeller pitch and diameter will vary according to the specific power output of various engines of the same capacity, and will also depend upon the airspeed at which any given model design may be intended to travel.

Engine Capacity	Running-in	Free Flight Sport
·5– ·8 cc	7×4	7 ×4
1·0– 1·5 cc	8×4	8 ×4
2·5– 3·5 cc	9×6	$8\frac{1}{2}$×5
5·0– 6·0 cc	11×6	10 ×4
8·0–10·0 cc	11×6	11 ×6

Engine Capacity	Competition Free Flight	Stunt or Sport Control Line
·5– ·8 cc	6×4	6×4
1·0– 1·5 cc	7×4	8×4
2·5– 3·5 cc	8×4	8×6/$8\frac{1}{2}$×5
5·0– 6·0 cc	10×4	10×6
8·0–10·0 cc	10×6	11×6

15 : Fuels

THE fuel formulae given below are good basic fuels for general running. For high performance many additives can be incorporated, and for very tight new engines it may be advisable to increase the oil content. Vintage fixed compression diesels, such as the Vivell ·06 and Drone Bee, often require a greater percentage of oil in the mixture.

All model aero engine fuels are made up of various components, each of which has an important part to play in the combustion process. With a two part petrol engine fuel formula the 75% petrol is ignited, in vapour form, and provides the power, while the 25% oil is for lubrication. A small proportion of Ether is sometimes added, and although this will help starting, particularly under cold conditions, it is not found to increase the power output. With glow engines, a Castor base oil, preferably de-gummed, such as Castrol M, acts as lubricant, while the Methonal content provides power, when burnt, and an additive, such as Amyl acetate acts as a mixing catalyst, but does not increase power output. The Methonal reacts with the platinum of the glow plug element, and the resultant chemical action, has a catalytic effect, which keeps the plug glowing. With diesel fuel, the Ether explodes under compression, the paraffin burns, and is a cheap source of power output, while the oil content is purely for lubrication purposes. The above explanations are a gross over simplification of the full facts, but should prove useful when considering the respective components of fuel mixtures.

Basic Petrol Formula:

- 25%   SAE 50/70 oil (or special 2-stroke oil).
- 75%   Low octane petrol.

Basic Glow Formula:

- 25%   Castor oil, or Castor-based de-gummed oil.
- 75%   Methonal.
- +4%   Nitro Methane*
- +1%   Amyl Acetate†

Basic Diesel Formula:

- 50%   Paraffin.
- 30%   Ether (use BP and not commercial).
- 20%   Caster oil or 20/50 SAE mineral oil.
- +2½% Amyl Nitrate (not essential, but a good anti-knock additive).

* Not essential but boosts power.
† Not essential but acts as a catlyst, and is specifically useful in very cold weather.

When mixing fuels it is essential to ensure that all components and mixing vessels are absolutely pure, and free from extraneous matter. It is advisable to filter the mixed-up fuel through filter paper. Remember that Ether and Nitro-Methane are highly volatile, and inflammable. They should always be stored in a cool dark place. Methonal has an affinity for water, and should only be mixed in a dry atmosphere, or it will be found that its volume has been increased by a substantial water content.

16: Timers, Tanks and Plugs

Engine Timers:

Many a good model has been lost, due to either the lack of a timer, or to a faulty one. The best timers have always been clockwork. Early clockwork timers were modified photo-timers. In 1975–76 SKB made one of the best mechanical clockwork units. Their airplane timer type-2 could be set to cut out between 10 and 22 seconds, and had a built in fuel cut off valve. The SKB type 1V which could be set between 5 and 30 seconds, is intended to squeeze a piece of silicone rubber fuel tubing, and so cut the fuel line. This type of timer is easily adapted to break the LT circuit on a petrol engine powered model, and one of these timers is in fact used to limit the engine run on the Brat ·14 powered Performance Kits Model L previously featured in Fig. 7. These timers can easily be adapted to operate the timer cut out arm of early diesel engines, such as the Mills 1·3 (Figs 60 and 61); this allows air to enter the fuel feed pipe before it enters the jet.

The airdraulic timer was pioneered by the Snip and later Elmic Timer Company in England. In America Austin-Craft produced a similar unit. Basically a spring loaded plunger forces air through a variable air valve. The rate at which the air is allowed to escape determines the cut-out time. The plunger is coupled to a fuel cut-off, or electric contact breaker, by varying the air valve adjustment screw; the time taken for the plunger to be forced down its cylinder is varied, and this is directly proportional to the length of engine run.

Fuel Tanks:

Most early petrol and diesel engines were supplied with a fuel tank, in unit with the engine. With side port motors it was usually affixed to the underside of the choke tube. A particularly neat example is given with the plated metal tank supplied with the Hurleman Aristocrat, which is illustrated in Fig. 14. In many instances the cut-out valve was inserted between the needle and the intake port, and this method is used with the Amco ·87 Mk 1, K Hawk and K Eagle motors. See Figs 70, 82, and 80. This either allowed air into the tube at this point, or blocked the intake tube with a plunger. With the Mills 1·3 engines, discussed earlier, fuel draw is destroyed by the ingress of air. The popular Mills ·75 was produced both with and without a cut-out. The latter model was intended for use with C/L models. The Mills 2·4 was fitted with a similar cut-out, but, being intended for C/L work, was not supplied with a tank. Most F/F orientated motors had a transparent plastic tank, so that the fuel level could easily be observed before launch. With the Atomatic 4·4 diesel, the tank was incorporated as part of the crankcase and formed an annular cavity around the crankshaft bearing housing. A similar, though transparent, arrangement was employed with the very rare MS 1·24 diesel. With some very early petrol engines a small, full size brass or copper carburettor float was used, as a separate entity, to act as a fuel tank. Messrs Hallam often favoured this simple tank arrangement. HP and Atlas engines always used a black plastic tank, which formed part of the carburettor unit, and was mounted below the choke tube.

With the advent of C/L flying it was found that, due to centrifugal force the old style fitted tanks no longer worked, as the fuel was thrown against the tank wall on the starboard side, and away from the fuel feed pipe; also due to the longer engine runs required their capacity was no longer adequate. To meet these problems special wedge shaped tanks were evolved with the feed tube at the back of the sharp end of the wedge. Feed and vent pipes were arranged so that the model could be flown inverted as easily as upright. Of historical interest, is the fact that some early C/L tanks were arranged so that the intake pipe rotated about the central axis of a cylindrical tank with a view to keeping the feed pipe, and the fuel, in immediate proximity. This system, although it worked, proved, with experience, to be expensive and unnecessary. Many stunt C/L flyers use a simple rectangular tank, with the feed pipe in the same position as the wedge tank, but with the feed and vent pipe outlets bent forward to face the slipstream. Anti-surge baffles are often incorporated with the larger stunt tanks, and these also serve to locate the inside end of the feed pipe.

For R/C, the tank capacity has to be increased again. For a ·61 cubic inch powered model an 8 fluid ounce tank is needed, and so what has been known as the clunk tank has evolved. These tanks are usually moulded in polyurethane, and the feed tube, about half of which is made of silicone rubber is weighted at its internal extremity, so that it clunks around the back of the tank, and always lies in the fuel. Care has to be taken to ensure that the fuel take up does not come into contact with the base of the tank (the end face) as this can restrict the fuel flow. A simple fine mesh wire gauze filter is often incorporated in the fuel feed system. If fitted these filters should be cleaned regularly to ensure that the engine does not fail in the air.

Plugs:

Except with very early petrol engines, most plugs are either $\frac{1}{4}$-inch or $\frac{3}{8}$-inch 32 tpi. Spark plugs were produced by Wipac, AC, KLG, OK, Maserati, Champion, Lodge, and Remco, as well as many other manufacturers. The Lodge plugs were particularly attractive and well made, featuring pink ceramic insulators and neatly knurled HT lead retaining nuts. Both long and short reach types were produced. In 1975 only OK and Remco spark plugs were still in production.

Glow plugs were made by Vulcan, KLG, OK, Johnson, DC, and Taipan, and of course many others. For R/C flying an 'idle bar' is sometimes fitted. The intention is to shield the element, during prolonged periods of idling, against rich mixture. High-class glow plugs have a coiled platinum element; inexpensive ones use a nickel alloy element. They are less efficient, and more prone to failure. Care should be taken to ascertain the correct reach plug for use with a given engine. The Vulcan plugs were available in a series of heat ranges for use with high Nitro content fuels as required for racing applications. The interesting OK plug was also fitted with a ceramic material, inside the plug body, and surrounding the element.

Long reach plugs can often be converted to short reach by the insertion of an extra plug washer.

17: Operating Tips

FOR running in, mount your engine in a plywood mounting rig. Bolt on securely with nuts, bolts and washers. As a general guide, for inclusive capacities of up to ·9 cc use 8 BA; ·9–4 cc use 6 BA; 4–10 cc use $\frac{1}{8}$ inch Whit. If finances permit use a DC Alloy adjustable test stand, which is suitable for engines of ·5–10 cc. *Never* put an engine directly in a vice.

Mount the fuel tank as near as possible to the engine, with the mean fuel level in the tank, level with the spray-bar. Keep Neoprene fuel tubing free of sharp bends, which might kink.

Check that the carburettor jet holes in the spray bar are correctly positioned in the venturi. If the spray bar is fitted with one hole this should point directly down the throat of the venturi. If it has two holes these should point against the sides of the venturi. In no case should one of these holes be directly visible when the spray bar is installed. Fit a suitable propeller for running-in purposes from the table in this book, featured in Chapter 14. The propeller should be fixed in such a way that for right hand flicking it is at the 2 o'clock position as it comes on compression, and the 8 o'clock position for left hand operation.

As a general rule, open the needle valve about $2\frac{1}{2}$ turns from the closed position and draw fuel from the tank by flicking with a finger over the air intake. Prime a few drops of fuel through the exhaust ports for initial starts from cold, and flick smartly. Use a rapid *wrist* action, not the arm. The engine should start within 3–4 flicks.

If trouble is experienced with a glow motor, check that the plug is glowing by looking through the exhaust port with the leads connected or remove the plug and examine. If the wire in the element is broken obtain a new plug. If the wire is in good order check the voltage of the accumulator ($1\frac{1}{2}$–2 volt) under load.

When the engine fires but will not run, open the needle valve gradually. If it runs and then cuts out, open needle. If engine fires but will not run while making 'squelchy' noises, close the needle and flick until the crankcase has cleared, as the engine is probably flooded. Blow out excessive fuel mixture through the exhaust ports. If the engine runs, 4-stroking, but throws out excessive mixture through the ports, close needle gradually. It should be remembered that it is much better to run an engine too rich than too lean, as the latter may cause overheating with consequential piston and liner burning, as well as overheating of the bearings.

With a diesel, general operation and needle valve adjustment is the same as for glow motors; however, there is the adjustment of the compression screw to be considered. Increase compression by screwing the adjusting screw down until the engine fires. Never screw down to a point where the propeller is difficult to turn over. As soon as the engine feels 'stiff', slacken off compression and fire contra-piston back against the end of the screw. If this is not done, damage will be done to the gudgeon pin and/or con-rod. As soon as the engine fires, increase compression slightly to keep it running, and then as the temperature builds up decrease it again gradually until the best running position is found.

If difficulty is experienced in starting a petrol engine, the trouble is nearly always faulty wiring joints, usually brought about by 'dry-soldering'. This is when a joint appears firm, but where the surfaces have been incorrectly cleaned, tinned and coated with flux. All connections must be checked and soldered very carefully. Petrol engines usually start with finger choking, and care must be taken not to flood them. Should this occur, remove the plug, blow excess fuel mixture from the plug points. Turn off the fuel with the needle, re-connect the HT lead to the plug, and resting the plug body on the cylinder head, flick the propeller smartly, and continue until a nice fat spark is seen to jump between the points. It will be noted that the engine will pump out excess fuel mixture through the plug hole and exhaust ports. When absolutely clear, re-insert the plug, open the needle about two turns, finger choke two or three times, turn on ignition, and the motor should start immediately.

Care should always be taken to check the continuity of the coil field windings with a new installation; this is to check that the primary and secondary windings have not shorted out. Great care should be exercised to avoid soldering wires to the coil, using too much heat, or for too long a time, as this may cause the connections on the inside of the coil winding tabs to come apart. It is also important to keep the contact points on the timer absolutely clean, and in perfect alignment. Draw a piece of clean stiff paper through the points to clear oil deposits. The point gap should be checked, using the maker's recommendations, with a feeler gauge. A volt meter put across the points should give a volt reading of $4\frac{1}{2}$ volt, assuming that this is the capacity used in the model. Needless to say, it is unwise to touch the HT lead when rotating the airscrew as an unpleasant shock can be received.

Most ignition systems use a $4\frac{1}{2}$ volt flat battery, and a large $4\frac{1}{2}$ volt booster is recommended for starting purposes. It is suggested that this should be wired into the ignition circuit via a socket and two way change-over switch. The engine timer is wired into the LT circuit. Start with the engine timer arm slightly retarded, and advance the ignition slowly, to the running setting, at the same time turning down the needle, until optimum performance is reached.

18: Cleaning, Overhauls and Restoration

Cleaning:

Whether an engine is required for use in an aircraft, or merely as a showpiece, forming part of a collection, it is important that it should be kept absolutely clean. Surface dirt can easily be removed by placing the engine in a small, previously cleansed, open tin (the author uses an individual pie tin), $\frac{3}{4}$ filled with paraffin. The engine should then be scrubbed with a stiff, good quality tooth brush, and subsequently dried and polished with a piece of torn up cotton sheet. After cleansing in this way, a few drops of Precision Oil should be inserted through the ports, and down the air intake. Steel parts such as compression screws etc., should be lightly smeared with oil.

For engines which have been run for considerable periods of time and have consequently built up a 'varnish' of burnt-on fuel and oil film, more drastic measures are necessary. It may be possible to remove this film by immersing the motor in commercial Carburettor cleaner and scrubbing with a tooth brush, or alternatively rubbing vigorously with Universal Cleaner, or even cellulose thinners, impregnated on a cotton cloth. Should the carburettor cleaner be used always wash the engine afterwards in the paraffin bath, as this cleaner is mildly acidic. Wash hands and eyes immediately with lots of water, should they become contaminated.

If the above methods have been utilised without avail on a particularly polluted engine, an even more effective procedure can be resorted to. This method is particularly effective for cleaning castings such as crankcases and cylinder heads, but does entail the complete dismantling of the motor. The part to be cleaned is placed in a small saucepan, which has been half filled with water and a strong concentration of household detergent washing powder. This is then brought to the boil, and the engine part suitably agitated with a wooden spoon, and scrubbed clean.

Particular care should be taken when cleaning O & R engines, as these are fitted with a cylinder head gasket which cannot be removed without great difficulty, and it is therefore not recommended that they should be cleaned other than by the paraffin method.

Overhauls:

An engine should *never* be dismantled, except by a competent mechanic, and then *only* when a specific repair job is to be undertaken. This is because, if a piston/liner unit is dismantled, the microscopic grooves, which have been worn in their mating surfaces, will not be exactly aligned when the motor has been re-assembled, and when run again, a further set of microscopic grooves will be imparted to these surfaces thus making the motor lose compression.

Having decided that it is essential to dismantle the motor, to effect some repair, firstly prepare a clean working surface, and cover it with clean paper. Ensure that all the correct tools are to hand; these should include a large selection of screwdrivers with both standard and Phillips head blades, together with parallel jaw and assorted snipe-nosed pliers, and, most important, a high quality leather strap wrench for removing polished cylinder heads and other circular polished alloy parts. On *no account* should any engine parts be put in a vice, except on rare occasions when they can be gently retained after the jaws have been carefully protected with copper or aluminium jaw pads. Many engines have been badly damaged, due to the fact that unthinking owners have clamped them in a vice by the outsides of their beam mounts. This usually distorts the crankcase, and at the least causes unsightly marking. The use of Mole wrenches should be strictly avoided.

When de-carbonising an engine, it is important never to use a steel scraper on the piston crown. Carbon should be gently removed, using a piece of close grained hardwood such as iron beech, and with an old motor it is advisable to leave a small ring of carbon around the periphery of the piston, as this helps the compression seal. When re-assembling, all parts should be carefully cleaned and oiled before re-assembly. Great care must be taken when tightening down cylinder head bolts, which should be tightened, a little bit at a time, crosswise over the head. Care should be taken to ensure that gaskets are in good condition and seating properly. New gaskets can be made by smearing the mating surface involved with oil, then using it as a die to make an impression on close grained paper or card material. This can subsequently be cut out using a craft tool.

A common fault when assembling engines, is not to check the correct position of the spray bar jet relative to the choke tube or venturi. If the spray bar has been drilled right through, and consequently has two jets, these should be arranged so that they face the walls of the tube or venturi, so that they are in the area of maximum airflow and minimum pressure, enabling the fuel mixture to be drawn out. If there is only one hole in the spray bar it must be arranged to face down the venturi or choke tube. If on inspecting an engine the spray bar jet is visible inside the intake tube, it will not run due to lack of fuel draw.

When bench testing the motor it is strongly advised that an alloy test bed, such as the DC unit, should be employed; alternatively a test bed can be made up by cutting an opening in a piece of high quality ply-wood about $\frac{3}{4}$ inch thick. Always use flat washers under the retaining nuts above the engine lugs, and below the bearers.

Restoration:

There are two ways in which a sickly engine can be restored. The first is to carry out an absolutely authentic restoration, using new or secondhand original parts, or alternatively to make exact duplicates of them, so that the completed motor exactly resembles the original motor in every way. The second method, which is quite satisfactory for flying purposes, is to replace missing or faulty parts with new, and sometimes superior substitutes, so that the restored engine is absolutely functional. Should this method be used, care should be taken not to modify any of the remaining original parts, and so make it difficult for an exact restoration to be carried out at a future date. A simple example of this is that should a non-standard needle valve assembly be fitted, and the spray bar be found to be of too great a diameter for the locating holes, on no account should the hole diameter be increased to accommodate the non-standard spray bar.

It is very satisfactory to see a completely scrap, or 'Bare Bones' as it is termed in America, engine restored to its former glory. Such a motor is the Majesco 4·5 petrol engine shown in Fig. 219. This motor has been completely restored by the expert toolmaker Mr L. Saxby. This Majesco had a damaged lower cylinder casting and was minus its crankcase rear cover, tank, and complete contact breaker assembly, and was generally in a very sorry condition before the restoration work was undertaken.

Many old engines, such as the HP Mk 3 diesel (Fig. 109) which have had a long and hard life, have suffered the indignity of having their mounting lug holes broken open, or in the case of extreme maltreatment, having their mounting lugs broken off altogether. Should this occur, the missing or broken parts can be built up with weld, and subsequently machined, and re-drilled, by an expert. The HP Mk 3 shown had two open mounting holes on one lug, and these have been superbly restored by Mr Saxby.

Some motors have anodised, stove enamelled or crackled crankcases or cylinder heads. These should always be restored to their original colours, and using as near original finish specifications as possible. For example, all Orwick engines had apple green enamel crankcases. (The almost identical Cunningham crankcases were enamelled blue.) The Yulon ·30, ·29 and ·49 motors had black crackle crankcases, although the Yulon Eagle had no exterior applied finish. Many K & B motors had green enamelled cylinder heads, and the 1975 Remco petrol engine is smartly finished with blue anodising on the head, tank, drive plate and points cover.

Steel contact breaker advance levers, which have been broken off inside delicate old castings, such as that used on the Stentor, can be removed by the use of a Spark Eroder.

Glossary of Technical Terms and Abbreviations

½A: Engines with a capacity of ·049 cubic inch.
Allen Key: A hardened metal key used to locate one metal object against another.
Anodising: The process by which an anti-oxidising layer of thin coloured metal is deposited over another metal.
BB: Ball-bearing.
Beam Mount: The method of affixing the engine on parallel hard wood beams, located in the fuselage.
BDC: Bottom Dead Centre, lowest point of piston travel.
Big-end: The larger end of the connecting rod, which encircles the crank pin.
Booster Battery: A large capacity battery, supplementary to the aircraft's, for starting.
Boost Port: An extra induction port used with Schnurle Porting, located opposite the exhaust port, and inclined upwards.
Bore: The diameter of the cylinder liner.
BR: Ball Race; a bearing incorporating hardened steel balls cased in position.
bhp: Brake Horse Power.
C/L: Control Line, method of controlling a power model, usually incorporating two steel control wires, together with a bell crank and control horn.
Clack Valve: A flat metal valve, admitting mixture to the engine when opened due to a lower pressure in the crankcase than that of the atmosphere.
Class A: Engines not exceeding 2·5 cc capacity.
Class B: Engines not exceeding 5 cc capacity.
Classic Engines: Engines combining quality, design and originality with aesthetic appeal.
Compression Ratio: This is the ratio of the cylinder volume, above the cylinder crown in the bottom dead centre position, to the unswept volume above the crown in the TDC position.
Con-rod: The connecting rod which joins the gudgeon pin to the crank pin.
Contact Breaker: The unit, incorporating contact points, which makes and breaks the low tension circuit, for a petrol engine.
Contra-piston: A piston fitted to form the cylinder head of a compression ignition engine. It can be moved up and down the cylinder to vary compression.
D: Diesel.
Die Casting: The technique by which castings are made, usually under pressure, with a metal die.
Drive Plate (or disc): Metal disc, affixed to front of crankshaft, which drives the propeller.

Drum Valve Induction: A fuel induction system, whereby the mixture enters the engine via a port in a rotating drum.

FAI: Federation Aeronautique Internationale, the international body governing model aeronautics.

F/F: Free Flight.

Flux: A liquid or paste used when affixing solder to metal.

FRV: Front Rotary Valve, an induction system incorporating a port cut into a hollow crankshaft.

G: Abbreviation for Glow, or glow engine.

Gasket: A thin washer made from paper, fabric or metal, used to seal one metal surface against another.

Gravity Casting: A casting made by simply pouring liquid metal into a mould, without the application of external pressure.

Gudgeon Pin: A steel rod connecting the little end of the con-rod to the piston skirt (called a wrist pin in USA).

High Spot: A raised spot on the piston or cylinder liner causing a poor cylinder liner/piston fit, and consequent overheating.

HT: High Tension.

Hydulignum: A multi-laminated resin-bonded wood, used for propeller manufacture.

IAECS: International Aero Engine Collectors Society.

Little End: The small top end of the con-rod, through which the gudgeon pin passes.

LT Circuit: Low Tension Circuit, as applied to model petrol engines, usually employing a $3-4\frac{1}{2}$ volt power source.

MECA: Model Engine Collectors Association (American based).

Methonal (or Methile): Alcohol, used as the burning ingredient for glow plug fuel.

Nitro-Methane (or Nitrated Methonal): Used as an additive to increase the power output for use with glo-plug engines.

N/V: Needle Valve, the valve used to regulate fuel input to the spray bar.

P: Petrol.

Phillips Head: A screw featuring a + type head, which is indented from the top.

Pitch: The horizontal distance that a propeller would move forward if it did not slip when turning in the air.

Plug Reach: The depth to which a plug screws into a cylinder head.

Radial Mount: Part of the engine, or separate accessory, which enables an engine to be mounted against a vertical fire wall in an aircraft.

Radial Port: Ports with openings arranged around the circumference of a circle.

R/C: Radio Control.

Rear Cover: The casting or plate which covers the back of the crankcase.

Rich Running: When an excess of fuel is fed to the engine, and surplus unburnt fuel is seen to proceed from the exhaust ports, with consequent 4-stroke running.

ROG: Take off's, Rise Off Ground.

rpm: Revs per minute.

Rotary Shaft Valve: Usually fuel induction via a port in a rotating hollow crankshaft.

Rotary Disc Induction: An induction system where the fuel mixture is controlled by a rotating disc, which is driven from the crank pin.

Schnurle Port: A porting system whereby the transfer ports direct the incoming gases away from a single exhaust port. Often used in conjunction with a Boost Port.

Side Port (SP): An induction system whereby the fuel mixture is directly controlled by an induction port, opened and closed by the piston.

Slag Engine: An engine, often of low quality, which is not fitted with a cylinder liner.

Sludge: The residue left in a model aero engine or fuel tank after the more volatile ingredients have evaporated.

SMAE: Society of Model Aeronautical Engineers.

Spinner Nut: A propeller retaining nut, machined to resemble a spinner.

Spray Bar: A hollow tube forming part of the carburettor—a hole is drilled in it to coincide with the venturi intake. One end contains the needle valve and the other is affixed to the fuel feed pipe.

Stroke: The distance which a fixed point on the piston travels between TDC and BDC.

Sub Piston Induction: Where the skirt of the piston is arranged to clear the lower surface of the exhaust port and so allow air to enter the crankcase below the piston.

Surface Jet: Where the spray bar or induction jet opening is flush with the side of the venturi.

TDC: Top Dead Centre. When the piston is at the top of its stroke.

Torque: A tendency for a model to rotate in the opposite direction to its propeller. An engine developing high torque characteristics can swing a large diameter propeller.

Transfer Port: An engine gas flow port, in the cylinder liner, transferring fuel mixture from the crankcase body to the combustion chamber.

Venturi: A tube which is progressively restricted towards a fixed point along its length, and then enlarged again. Thus a low pressure, high speed gas area is created at the point of restriction.

Vibramatic: A spring loaded clack induction valve.

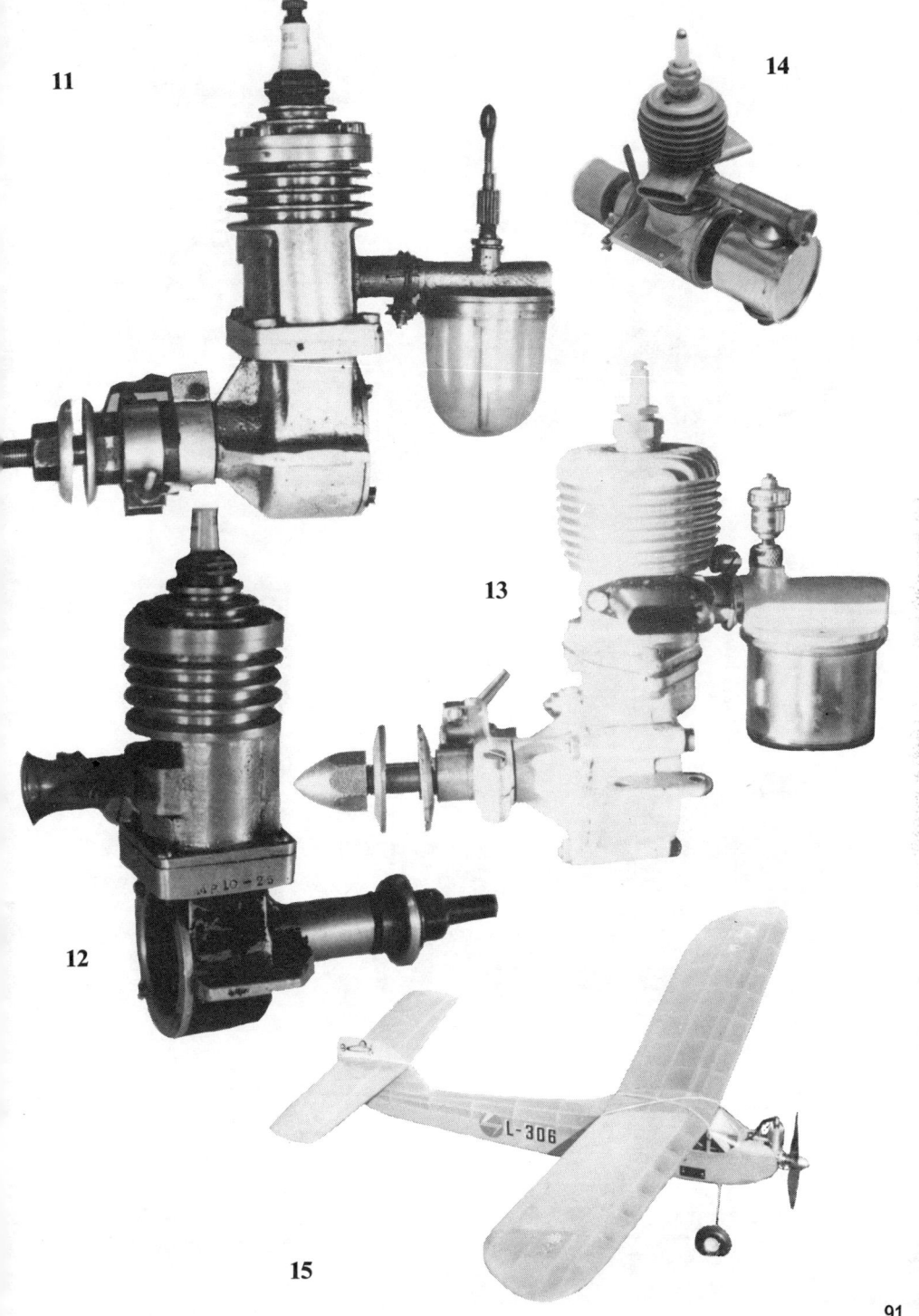

29

30

31

32

33

34

36

38

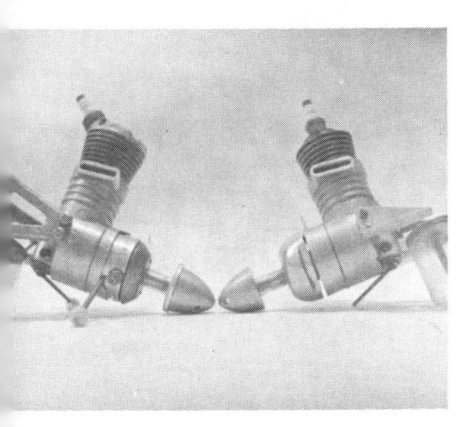

40

25

41

41a

42

43

44

46

50

52

53

54

55

56

57

59

60a

62

63

64

65

66

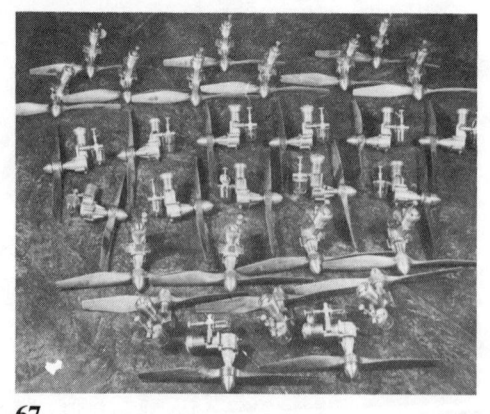

67

68

71

73

75

76

77

78

79

80

81

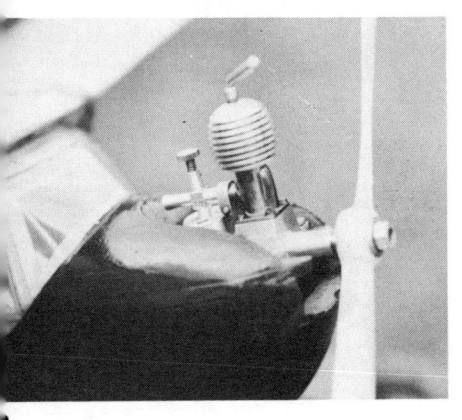

83

85

87

88

89

90

91

92

93

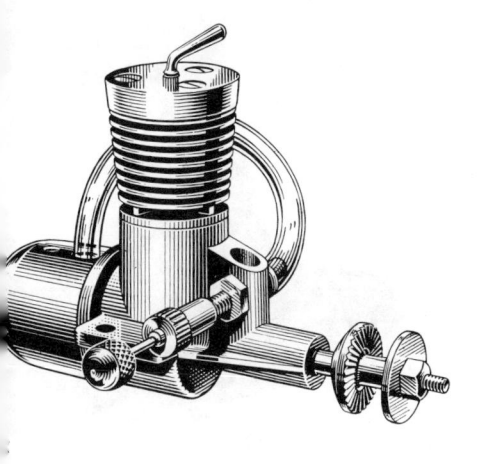

97

99

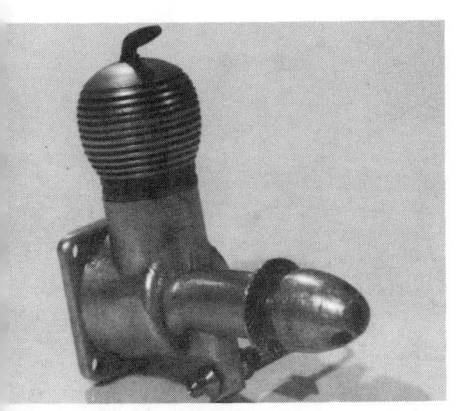

101

105

102

103

104

105

106

107

108

109

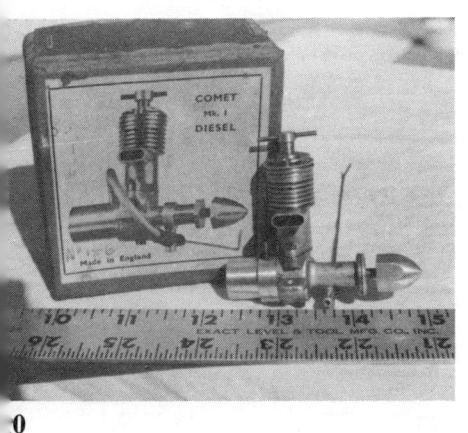

110

111

112

113

114

115

116

117

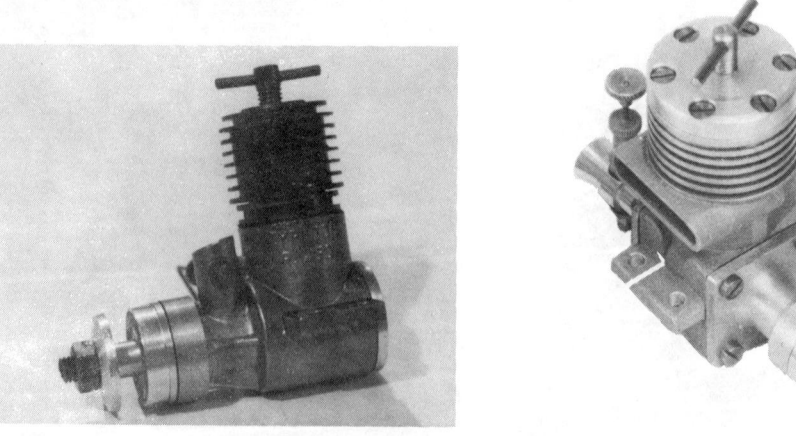

118   **119**

121

123

125

126

127

128

129

130

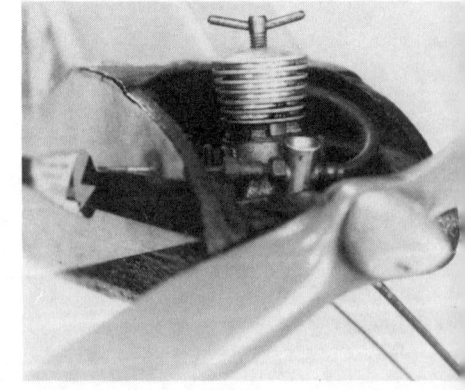

131

132

133

134

135

136

137

138

140

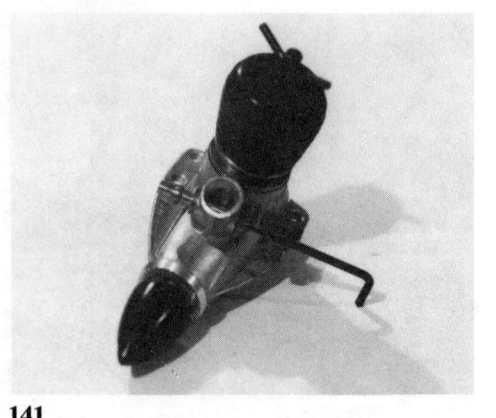

141

142

143

144

145

146

147

148

149

150

151

152

153

154

155

156

157

158

159

160

161

162

2a

178

181

182

183

184

185

186

187

188

189

190

191

192

193

194

195

196

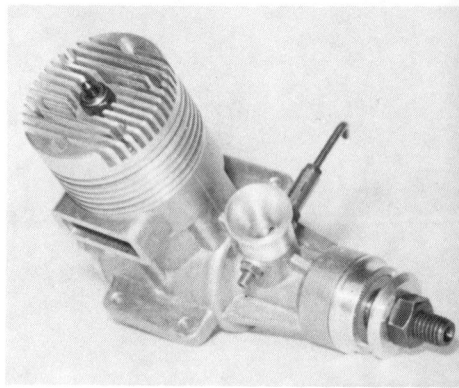
197

198

199

201

202

203

204

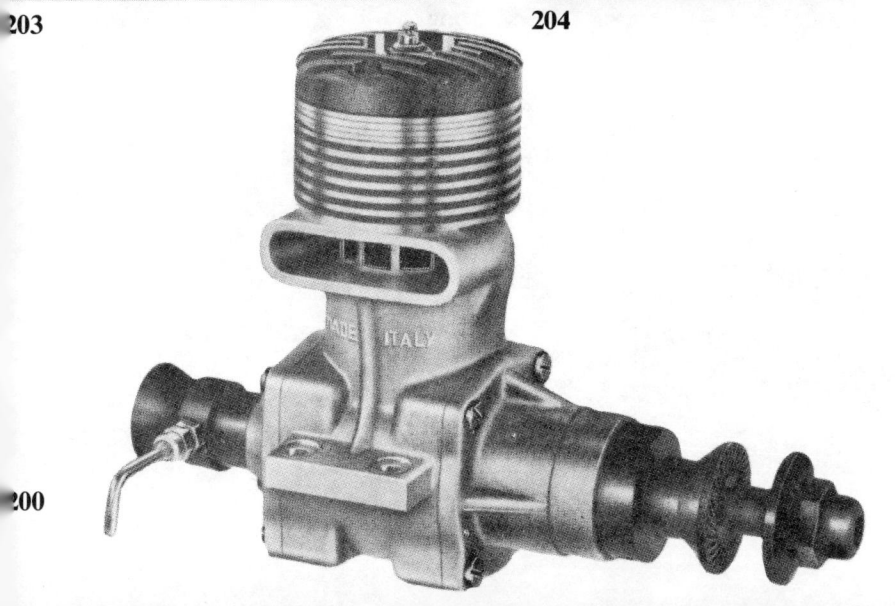

200

205

206

207

208

209

210

211

212

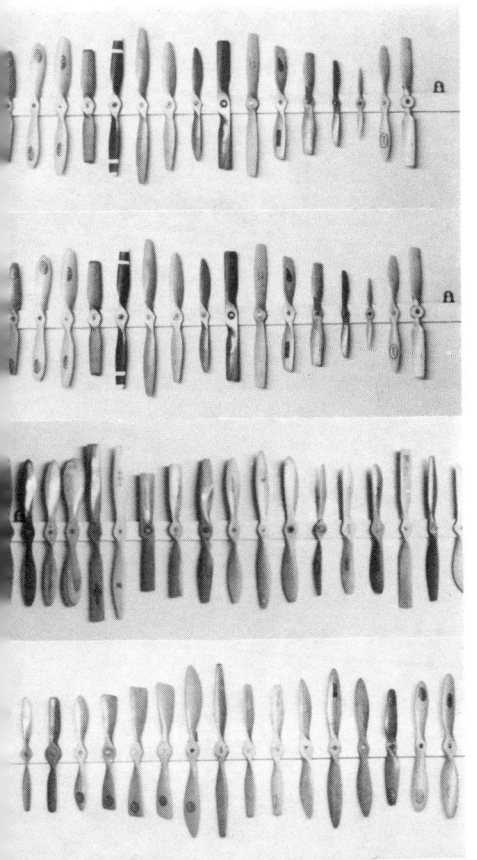

214

213

218

219

220

221

222

223

224

226

228

230

231

232

233

234

235

236

7

238

242

244

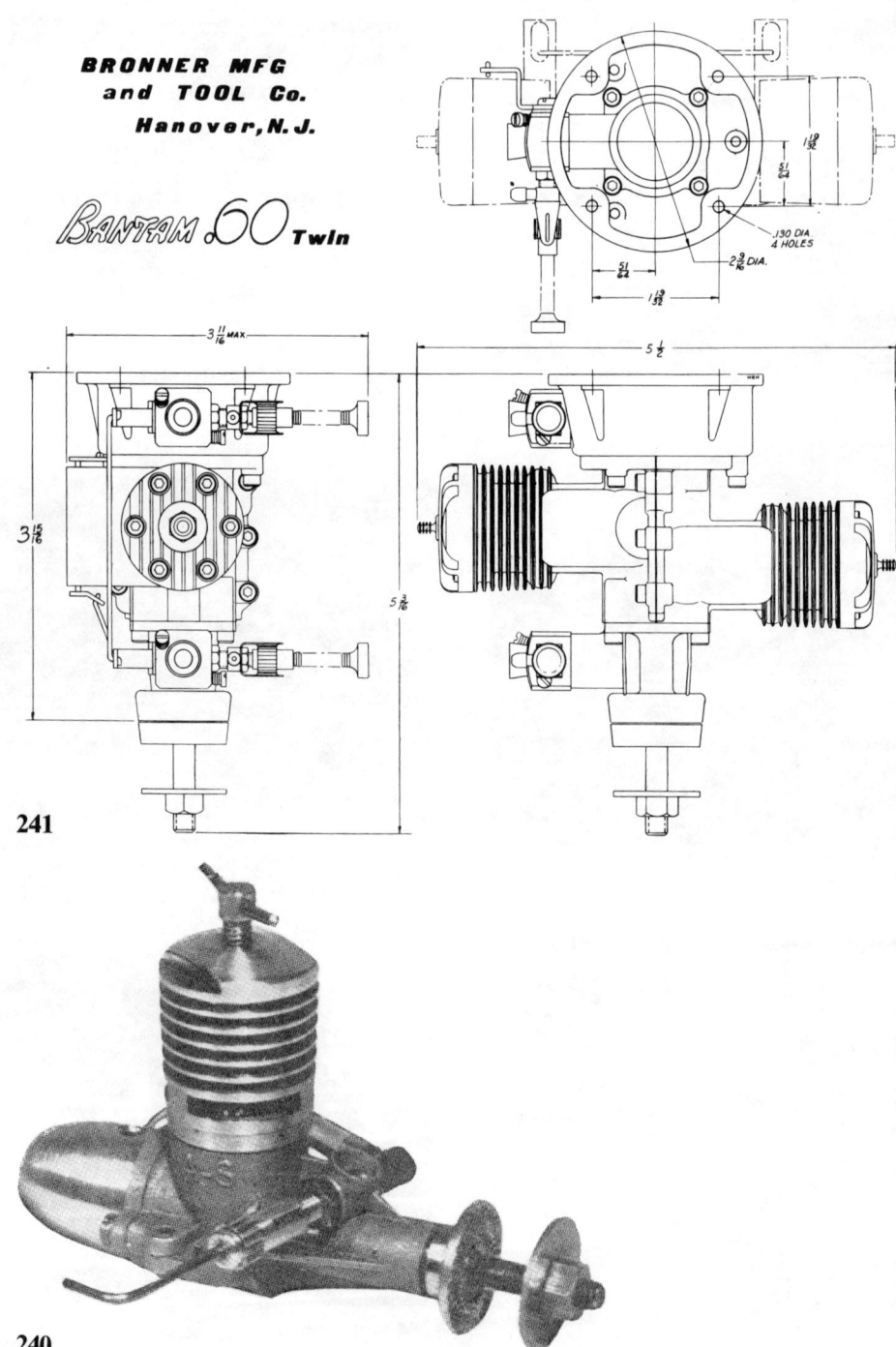

246

248

INDEX FOR ENGINES FEATURED

A denotes Compressed Air Engines
CO₂ denotes Carbon-dioxide Engines
D denotes Diesel Engines
E denotes Electric Engines
G denotes Glow Plug Engines
P denotes Petrol Engines
Italicised numerals denote figure numbers

Engine	Pages	Engine	Pages	Engine	Pages
Ace 0·5 D	41	Brown CO2	55, *172*	Davies-Charlton Manxman D	39, *107*
Aero ·35 G	57, *174*	Brown CO2 Twin	55	Davies-Charlton Merlin D	39
Aerol Gremlin D	38	Brown Junior P	12, 15, 55, 83	Davies-Charlton Rapier Mk 1 D	
Airo Mighty Midget P	16, *6*	BMP 3·5 D	41, *202*		39, *108*
Airplan 2·15 D	30	BMP ·9 D	41	Davies-Charlton Rapier Mk 2 D	40
Airplan 5·5 D	30, *244*	Boss Moran 3·5 D	35, *245*	Davies-Charlton Sabre D	40
Airstar 2·15 D	29, *56, 233, 239*	Boss Moran 5 D 35	35	Davies-Charlton Spitfire D	39
Alag X3 D	41	Buco ·60 G	53	Davies-Charlton Super Merlin	39
Alag ·25 D	41	Bunch D	28, 44	Davies-Charlton Tornado	52, *161*
Allbon Arrow G	61 *62*	Bunch Warrior P	*5*	Davies-Charlton Wildcat Mk 2 D	
Allbon Dart D	39	Bunch Tiger Aero P	*231*		39
Allbon Spitfire D	39, 40	Bungay ·60 P	65	Davies-Charlton Wildcat Mk 1 D	
Allbon Javelin D	39	Busek ·01 D	40		39, 61, 62
Allbon 2·8 D	39	Buzz P	25, 26	Davies-Charlton Wildcat Mk 3 D	
Alfa Mk 1	42	Buzz CO₂	55		40, 42, 62, *104*
Allyn	53, *171*			Davies-Charlton Wasp G	*183*
Alpha E	60	Cameron ·23 P	19, *206, 216*	Decca-Jet	56
A-M 10 D	45	Camm Flash	12	Deezil D	44, *132*
A-M 15 D	45	Camm Twin	49	Delmo 2·65 D	27
A-M 25 D	45, *145*	Campus CO₂	55	Delong 30 P	21, *35*
A-M 35 D	45	Cannon P	19, *224*	Dennymite P	17, *19*
Amco ·87 Mk. 1 D	34, 41, *70*	Carter 5 G	65	De-Za-Lux ZA92 D	38
Amco ·87 Mk. 2 D	34	Chunn Twin P	48	Diesella 2·4 D	32
Amco PB 3·5 D	34, 67, *71, 72*	Chunn Chum P	48	Drome Demon Mk 1	26
Amco BB 3·5 D	34, 45	C.I. Special P	24	Drome Demon Mk 2	26
Amro 10 G	72	Clan ·9 D	29	Dob-Ott A	13
Anderson Spitfire P		Clansman 5 D	41	Dooling ·29 G	65
	18, 20, 71, 83, *21*	Clipper Generator P	17	Dooling ·61 P	20, 65, 72, 83, *199*
Apex 120 P	72	Clipper Sky King P	17, *17*	Dragon 16 P	*243*
Apex Nipper D	46, *147*	Clipper XX770 P	17	Dragonfly ·01 D	40, 46
Aquilo Baby D	41	Cloud 3 P	29	Dragonfly Twin D	50
Arden ·199 P	19, 39, 61, 83, *29*	Comet Mk. 1 D	41, *110*	Drone Bee D	28, 76, *52*
A-S 55 D	40, 39, 61, 83, *240*	Comet Mk. 2 D	41	Dydesdyne D	41
Astral 5·9 P	16	Comet 18 P	74	Dyna-Jet	56, *173*
Aston A	13	Condor 4 P	50	Dyne 3 D	33
Astro Flight E	60	Condor Kopper King P	17, *18*	Dyne 2 D	33
Atlas 3·5 P	18, 16, 79, *9*	Contestor D60R P	23, *44*	Dyne 3·8 P	33
Atom ·09 P	22, *41*	Contestor SP P G	23, 16, 61	Dyno D	27, 72, 83, *48*
Atom 1A D	43, *120*	Cox G	53, 64		
Atom 1·8 D	43, *41A, 233*	Cox Colden Bee	55	ED Mk 2	27, 30, *57*
Atom Major 3·5	43	Cox-Hasa G	53	ED 2·49 Mk 3	36
Atom 6cc P	21	Craftsman P	49, *154*	ED 3·46	36, 66
Atom Minor 15cc P	21, *36*	Cunningham P	63	ED Baby ·46	36, *89*
Atom Super 1·8 D	43			ED Bee Mk 1	36, 37, *88*
Atomatic 4·4 D	43, 78	David-Anderson Drabant Mk 1 D		ED Bee Mk 2	37, *93*
Atomatic 1 D	42		42, *115*	ED Cadet	38
Atwood Cadet G	62, *184*	David-Anderson Drabant Mk 2 D		ED Comp Special	36, *87*
Atwood Wasp G	62		42, *116*	ED Fury	37
Autoplan A	13	David-Anderson Eccentric D	30	ED Hornet	37
Avion Mercury 45 P	17	David-Anderson Satellitt D	42, *117*	ED Hawk	38
		David-Anderson Tellus P	42	ED Hunter	37, *90*
Baby Cyclone P	17, 19, 20, 83, *20*	Davies-Charlton 350 Mk 1 D	39	ED Miles Special	37, 67, 70, *94*
Baby Engine P	11	Davies-Charlton 350 Mk 2 D		ED Pep	37, *95*
Ball ·604 P	65		39, *105*	ED Racer	37, 65, *91*
Bantam ·60 G	52, *241*	Davies-Charlton 350 Glow		ED Super fury	37, *92*
Barker P	21		39, 61, *106*	Eifflaender 2·5 D	67
BE-961 Twin D	73, *222*	Davies-Charlton Bantam G	40, 62	Elf Corn Cob P	49
Bensen Thorning P	31, *58*	Davies-Charlton Bambi D	39, *229*	Elf Four P/G	48, *155*
Brat ·14 P	16, 19, 71, 78, *7, 15*	Davies-Charlton Dart D	39	Elf Twin P	49
Bronner G	52	Davies-Charlton Eccentric D	40	Elf Six P	49
Brown Brownie P	15, *2*	Davies-Charlton Javelin D	39, 40		

Name	Page
Elfin 1·8 F/F D	38, 41, 99
Elfin 1·8 C/L D	38, 41, 98
Elfin 1·49 PB D	38
Elfin 2·49 Rad. D	38, 100
Elfin 2·49 PB D	38, 101
Elfin ·50 D	39
Elfin 1·49 BR D	39
Elfin 1·8 BR D	39
Elfin 2·49 BR D	39, 102
Embee ·75 Mk 1 D	44, 133
Embee ·75 Mk 2 D	45
Embee ·75 Mk 3	45, 58
Embee Twin D	45, 51, 136
Embee Mock Rotary D	58
Embee Glow Twin	53
Embee 2·5 D	45
Embee ·75 Mk 4 D	45, 135
Embee ·75 BR D	45
Embee 10 D	45, 134
Enya G	68
ERE D	66
Eta 5cc D	41, 111
Eta ·29 G	66, 67
Eta Elite D	41
Etha D	27, 218
Exeter 10 G	62, 181
Feeney 4-Cycle P	24
Fireball 500 P	19
Fisher 3·5 D	46, 149
FMO 3·5 Little Boxer D	51, 69, 157
FMO 5cc Boxer D	51, 69
FMO 6cc Boxer D	61, 69
FMO 9·2 Boxer D	51
FMO 7·5 Boxer G	53, 169
FMO 8·2 Boxer G	53
FMO 10cc Boxer G	53
FMO 16cc Boxer G	53
Forster ·99 P	72
Forster ·29 P	21
Foursome 1·2 D	40
Fox ·35 G	63
Frog 175 P	34, 73
Frog 100 D	34, 74
Frog 180 D	34
Frog 160 G	61, 179
Frog 250 D	34
Frog 500 D	62, 180
Frog 500 P	61
Frog 150 RD	34
Frog 349 D	34
Frog 80 D	34, 77
Frog 50 D	34, 76
Frog 249 BR D	35
Frog 149 Vibra-Matic D	34, 75
Frog Venom 1400 G	35
Frog Viper 1500 D	34, 78
Frog Venom ·049 G	35, 62
Frog 049 RG	34
Fuji G	68
Gamage P	11
Gannet P	23, 24, 45
Gannet 30cc Twin	24
GB 50 D	28
GB 50 G	28
GB 75	28
GB 750	28, 29
Gee Bee Stunta-Mota D	28
Genie	25
G.H.G. 4·4 P	16, 33, 10
G.H.G. 4·4 G	33, 64, 128
G.H.G. Twin P	33, 49, 65
G.H.G. 1·5 D	33
G.H.G. 2·4 D	33, 66, 67
G.H.Q. P	26
Giglio 2cc D	27
Gilbert ·07 G	63, 186
Gilbert ·11 G	63
Glo-Chief ·29 G	29, 64, 194
Glo-Chief ·35 G	29, 64
Glo-Chief ·49 G	29, 64
Glo-Chief ·35 BB G	64, 195
Glo-Chief ·19 R/C G	68
Golden Eagle ·56 P	19
GP 1·5 D	32
GP 100 D	32
Grayson Gnome 3·5 P	15
Grayson Greyspec 15cc P	15
Grayson 25cc P	24
Grayson 30cc P	24
Hallam 2·5 D	46
Hallam Conqueror ·60 P	16, 78, 4
Hallam Nipper P	19, 78
Hargreave G	24
Hastings 1066 Falcon P	18, 24
HB ·61	68
Hetherington Meteor ·23 P	22, 61, 83, 38
Hetherington Meteor ·23 G	61, 178
H & H ·45	61
H & H ·38 Twin	50
Hobbs ·75 D	72 220
Holland Hornet ·049 G	62
Holland Hornet ·51 G	62
Holland Hornet ·51 R/C G	62
Hoosier Whirlwind A	13 14, 1
Hornet ·61 P	20, 64
Hornet ·19 G	225
Howie Twin	50
Howler ·61 P	22, 40
HP Mk 2 P	16, 41, 203
HP Mk 3 D	41, 78, 86, 109
HP ·61 R/C G	68
HP ·40 R/C G	68
Hurleman Aristocrat P	16, 78, 48
Hurleman ·60 P	15
Husky Junior	19
Imp A	13
J. B. Atom 1·5	44, 45, 131
J. B. Bomb 1 D	44, 45
Jena 1cc D	45, 35, 137
Jena 2cc D	45, 138
Jena 2·5cc D	45, 139
Jetex 300 J	59, 177
Jetex 100 J	59
Jetex 150 J	59
Jetex Scorpion J	59
Jetex 50 J	59
Joe Ott A	13
Johnson ·29 G	61, 63, 66
Johnson ·32 G	63
Johnson ·35 G	63
Johnson Stunt Supreme G	63, 76, 83, 189
Judco	25
Judco Ram	21, 25, 26
Juggernaut J	56
K. Eagle D	35, 78, 80
K. Falcon D	36, 84
K. Kestrel D	36, 62, 83
K. Tornado G	36, 62
K. Vulture Mk 1 D	36, 85
K. Vulture Mk 2 D	36
K. Vulture Mk 3 D	36, 86
K. 6 P	16, 13
Kamikaze	43, 53, 170
K & B 201 G	64, 86, 193
K & B ·29 P	61, 71
K & B ·40	69
K & B Infant G	62
K & B ·32	57
Kemp Hawk Mk 1 D	35, 78, 235
Kemp Hawk Mk 2 D	35, 82
Kemp 1·9	35, 81
Kemp 4·4	35, 79
Kemp 8·8 Twin D	35
KK CO_2	55
Kolbe Rhino G	69, 215
Komet 10	72
Kyowa ·45 R/C G	68
Larson Royal 105 G	26
Lee In-Line Single	57
Leesil 2·5 D	27
Letna	43
Lionheart 2·5 D	58, 176
Lauterel P	26
Lyon MP 5 P	16, 11
Lyon MP 10 P	16, 12
Mabuchi Aeromotor E	60
Mac C	57
Madewell Twin P	50
Majesco 2·2 D	32, 40
Majesco 4·5 P	18, 32, 40, 86, 25, 219, 234
Majestco Mite D	32, 95
Masco Buzzard	46
Mattel E	66
May Rocket ·56 P	23
May Silver King P	23
McCoy ·60 P	64
McCoy ·29 P	232
McCoy D	38, 97
ME Heron 1cc D	38, 96
ME Snipe 1·5 D	38
ME Snipe R/C D	38, 69
MEC 1·2 D	41
Mechanair P	16, 8
Melcraft P	35
Merco ·60 G	68
Meteor Maraget D	45
Micro ·8	223
Micron ·29 G	18, 64, 22
Micron 5cc D	28
Micron ·8cc D	45
Micron 2·5 D	45
Micron 2·5 BR D	68, 144
Micron 2-24 G	52, 167
Micron 4-24 G	52, 83, 168
Micron ·35 R/C	69, 208
Micron ·45 G	20, 209
Micron M-2-24 Bi-Cylindre	69
Micron ·56 G	64
Micron M-29 G	64
Micron M-35 G	64
Micron M-49 G	64
Micron ·21 G	69, 210
Micron ·9cc G	45, 143
Micron Meteor 51A G	64, 197

Milford Mite D	 26	Pepperill 28	Synchro Ace ·562 P 25
Mills Mk 1 1·3 D		Perky P 22, 39	Synchro Bee ·122 25
	32, 74, 78, 60, 60A	Pfeffer D 43, 123	Synchro B-30 25
Mills Mk 2 1·3 D	32, 41, 78, 61	Pierce J 21	Synchro PC-2 25
Mills ·75 Mk 1 D	32, 78, 83, 230	Pierce R 21, 37	
Mills ·75 Mk 2 D	32, 78, 83, 62, 64	P.K. Panther V-Twin 51, 158	Taifun Hobby Mk 1 D 45, 140
Mills 2·4 D	.. 33, 78, 63		Taifun Hobby Mk 2 D 45, 141
Mills Doonside ·75 D	18, 71, 212	Queen Bee ·23 P .. 20, 31	Taifun Hurrikan D .. 39, 103
Mills Indian ·75 D	.. 72, 213	Queen Bee ·60 P 20	Taifun Rasant D .. 45, 142
M & M	 23	Queen Bee ·60 G 20	Taifun Orkan 45
M & M Hurleman Twin ·96 P			Taifun Zyklon 45
	50, 228	Rawlings R-18 D 27, 30, 31, 83, 49	Taipan 1·5 D 29, 43, 128
Moki 25cc G ..	.. 69, 215	Rawlings R-30 D 27, 30, 31, 50	Taipan Tyro D 29
Monsun Standard	 32	Raylite Panther D .. 46, 67	Taipan ·61 G 68
Morin D	 46	Rapier 1cc 46	Taipan ·15 Schneurle G 68, 238
Morton Burgess M-5 P	24, 49, 46	Reeves 6cc P 18, 40	Taipan 3·5 Schneurle G 43, 68
Motop Mk 16 D	.. 43, 125	Reeves 3·5cc D 40	Taipan 2·5 BR D .. 43, 68
MS 1·24 D	.. 35, 79	Reeves H 18 D 40	Taplin Twin D .. 51, 69
MS 2·5 D	.. 29, 247	Reeves Goblin D 40	Telco 55, 172A, 196, 204
MVVS 1·5 D ..	.. 43, 121	Remco ·29 P 71, 86, 211	TFA 72
MVVS 2·5 D ..	 67	Rythm 2·5 .. .. 43, 127	Tiger-Jet 56
		Rivers Silver Streak D 44, 67	Thimble Drome G 64
New Atom Minor 6cc P	.. 21	Rivers Silver Arrow D 44, 129	Thor ·29 P 25, 47
Nomie A ..	 13	Rocket ·451 Victor P .. 23, 43	Thuella Favoriet 2·47 D 43, 66, 205
Nordec G & P	.. 65, 198	Rocket 4610 P 23	Tlush Super Ace P 72
Northfield-Ross ·61 In-Line G		Rogers KD-29 25	Tono ·35 R/C G .. 68, 207
	52, 162	Rogers ·29 & ·35 25	Typhoon R-250 D .. 42, 118
Northfield-Ross ·61 Flat Twin G		Rogers RMC-2 25	Typhoon 5cc D .. 42, 67, 119
	52, 163	Rogers ·29 ('46 Mod) .. 25	Typhoon 7cc Twin D 42, 159
Northfield-Ross Flat 4 G	52, 164	Rogers Ram 25	Typhoon 2·47 PB 42
Northfield-Ross Flat 6	52, 165	Rossi ·60 G 55, 66, 200	Typhoon Mk 4 42
		Rossi-Vulcan Jet 56	Typhoon Super 10cc G .. 42
O.K. Cub ·19 G	.. 62, 182	Ross-Power Custom ·61 G .. 69	
O.K. ·049 G ..	 62	Rowell ·60 64	Ueda G 69
O.K. ·60 P	 221	Ruppert Twin D .. 51, 160	
O.K. ·35 G	 62		Vasteras 2·06 D 72
O.K. Twin P ..	48, 74, 83, 151	Sabre ·29 G 64	Veco ·32 G 57
O.K. Cub CO₂	 55	Sabre ·35 G 64	Vertorek D 43, 126
Oliver Tiger D	.. 44, 46, 67	Sampson ·30 P 21	Viking 2·5 G 63, 187
Oliver Cun D ..	 44	Savage ·60 P 57	Viking Twin 65 P .. 48, 52, 153
Oliver Major D	 44	Saxby ·375 D 46, 148	Vivell ·06 D 28, 76, 53
Oliver Twin	 44	Saxby ·5 D 46, 148	Vivell ·35 P 19, 44, 28
O.P.S. 40 G ..	.. 66, 69	Scout Twin P 48	Vulcan 55
ORR Tornado ·65	 226	Shershaw ·60 .. .. 52 53	
O & R Midget G	.. 62, 185	Sky-Fury G 53	Warrior P 12
O & R ·23 SP P	19, 83, 84, 27	Smith Lapwing P .. 16, 18, 16	Wasp Twin P 48, 152
O & R ·23 FRV P	.. 19, 26	Sona Jet 56, 173	Wasp Soecial Twin P 48
O & R 60 Spec. P	16, 84, 3	Sparey 5cc D 28	Webra 1·5 D 38
O & R Gold Seal P	 83	Speed Demon 30 .. 47, 150	Webra Mach 1 D 68
Orwick ·64 P ..	.. 18, 86	Stanger V-4 P 11	Webra Twin D 51
Orwick ·35 G ..	 63	Stanger V-2 P 11	Westbury Kestrel P .. 21, 34
OS G ..	 63	Stanger 3-Cyl. P 11	Weston CO₂ 55
OS Jet ..	.. 56, 173	Stentor 6cc P .. 18, 86, 23, 248	Weston 3cc D 35
OSAM D ..	.. 42, 112	Strato Diesel ·604 .. 28, 54	Weston Stunt 3·5 D 35
OTM Kolibri ·8cc	.. 43, 124	Strato ·604 P 20, 28, 32	Wisard Twin G .. 52, 166
Ott Favorite A	 13	Streamline 6 P 227	
Ott-Norlipp A	 13	Strong 48, 53	X- ULT 0·375 D .. 45, 246
Ouragan 3·36 D	 29	Stuart Turner P 12	
Ouragan ·9 D ..	.. 29, 83, 55	Super Cyclone P 18, 20, 71, 33	Yulon ·30 G 63, 64, 86, 190
Owatt D	.. 29, 51	Super Elia P 42	Yulon ·29 G 63, 86, 191
		Super Sokal D .. 46, 146	Yulon ·49 G 63, 86
Pagco ·09 G ..	.. 63, 188	Super-Tigre X -40 G 69	Yulon Eagle G .. 63, 86, 192
PAL ·55 P	.. 53, 156	Super-Tigre G 30 D .. 42, 114	Yulon 2·5 D 63
PAL ·55 CG	 53	Super-Tigre G 32 D .. 42, 69, 113	
PAL 110	 53	Super-Tigre X.. .. 43, 69	ZN ·60 P 64
PAW 1·5 D	.. 46, 67, 242	Super-Hurricane P .. 19, 30	Zom 2·5 D 44, 130
PAW 2·5 D	..67, 122, 242	Super Wasp Twin P 48	
PAW 3·5 D	.. 67, 242	Synchro Ace Special ·562 P .. 25	